TITANIC
TRAGEDY

VINCENT McDONNELL

The Collins Press

Published in 2007 by
The Collins Press
West Link Park
Doughcloyne
Wilton
Cork

A Cataloguing-In-Publication Data record for this book is available from the British Library

ISBN: 978-1905172412

Typesetting: The Collins Press

Font: Optima, 14 point

Printed in Ireland by Colourbooks Ltd.

CONTENTS

1

DOWN IN THE DEEP

Four thousand metres beneath the Atlantic Ocean lies the wreck of a great ship. It is a dark, silent world down there. Its only inhabitants are fish and creatures of the deep. Almost 100 years has passed since the ship sank. In that time, only a handful of people have ever descended to the wreck and seen its watery grave.

Yet the rusting remains hold an enduring interest that has not lessened since it sank on a cold, April night in 1912. For, despite the thousands of ships which have sunk since man first sailed the oceans of the world, this one lying deep beneath the Atlantic is the most famous of all of them.

It still holds a special mystery and fascination, which shows no sign of fading. In fact, its fame has increased through the years. Today, people still speak of it with awe. Many books have been written about it, as have songs and poems, and Hollywood has made films about it.

Yet it was a young ship when it sank. It was on its first, or maiden, voyage across the Atlantic. It was sailing to New York from Cobh, County Cork, then known as Queenstown.

The ship sank on a calm, cold, starry night. Its fate was decided in less than 60 seconds. One moment it was sailing majestically through the darkness, with all its light ablaze. Then an iceberg was sighted dead ahead.

A warning bell peeled in the darkness. The ship's wheel was spun hard-a-starboard. But it was too late. The ship's hull collided with an underwater section of the iceberg. Minutes later, its lights still ablaze, the stricken ship lay motionless in the water. Its fate was sealed and it was doomed to die.

Already the dark waters of the Atlantic Ocean were gushing in through a gash torn in its side by the collision. In less than three hours the largest ship ever built would break in two. Its bow and stern would then sink slowly beneath the waves.

The ship, built in Belfast and described as unsinkable, was to become a grave for the 1,503 men, women and children who drowned in the tragedy. Of the 2,208 passengers and crew on board that April night, only 705 survived to tell the story of what happened.

It is a story of foolishness and rash stupidity. It is a story of man's greed, pride and ambition. It is also a story of heroism, bravery and sacrifice, and of terrible cowardice. It is a story of chance and of the many lives and dreams that were destroyed, and a story of the families who were separated by the tragedy.

Some of the men and women who survived were hailed as heroes. Many of those who perished did so heroically. But many men behaved in a shameful, cowardly manner that night. They lived out their lives in disgrace, aware that in saving themselves they had left others to their fate. Many of those left to drown were women and children.

The ocean, however, is an indifferent entity. It does not care who lives or dies, whether they are young or old, male or female, rich or poor. It will accept them all and take them to a watery grave.

Many of their names are still remembered today. The names Bruce Ismay, Sir Cosmo and Lady Duff-Gordon, Robert Hitchens and Major Peuchen, have become associated with cowardice.

Others, like Thomas Andrews, Benjamin Guggenheim, Colonel Archibald Gracie, Ida Straus, Molly Brown and twelve-year-old Ruth Becker are remembered for their bravery and courage that night.

This is the story of that fateful night. This is the story of those men, women and children who lived and those who died. This is a story of heroism, cowardice and great sacrifice.

It is also the story of one of the finest and most famous ships ever to sail the seas, why she was built and the men who built her. The story also tells how she now lies silent and rusting beneath the Atlantic waves.

Her name is *Titanic* and this is her story.

2
THE NEW WORLD

From the beginning of time man has been fascinated by the sea. He has stood on the shores of the world's oceans and watched the ceaseless movement of the water. He has gazed out towards the horizon and wondered what lay beyond that line where the sky joined the sea.

Curiosity has been part of the driving force of humankind. It was this curiosity that made men determined to discover what lay on the other side of the great oceans. Driven by their desire to know, men took to the oceans in boats and travelled beyond the horizon.

These first boats were built of wood and propelled by paddles. Later sails were added which harnessed the power of the wind. In places where wood was scarce, rafts were built from bundles of reeds lashed together. Boats were also constructed from wooden frames covered with animal hides and sealed with pitch.

In these flimsy craft, men traversed the oceans. Around the middle of the sixth century, Saint Brendan, the Navigator, sailed from Ireland to many of the islands off the Scottish coast. Legend has it that he sailed to America in his flimsy leather boat 800 years before Christopher Columbus.

Leif Ericsson, the great Norse explorer, is also credited with having reached America around 1,000AD. The remains of what are thought to be a Viking settlement were discovered in Newfoundland in 1963. But there is no absolute evidence that Saint Brendan or Leif Ericsson ever reached America.

What is fact is that Christopher Columbus reached what we now know as the West Indies in 1492. He had been seeking a new route to India but instead discovered what was to become known as the New World.

It was this discovery that was to lead to the building of *Titanic*, more than 400 years later. Like Columbus' own ship, the *Santa Maria*, the *Titanic* was destined to become one of the most famous ships ever to sail the seas.

Following in the footsteps of Columbus, others sailed to this New World from Spain, Portugal and England. It was from one of these men, Amerigo Vespucci, allegedly the first European to set foot on the mainland, that this New World got the name America.

These adventurers brought back stories of a vast land. It was a land where a man could become rich beyond his wildest dreams. These dreams in turn fired the imagination of many other adventurers and they too travelled to America seeking their fortunes.

The vast Atlantic Ocean lay between Europe and the new land of America. The only means of travelling there was by ship. These ships were built of wood and had sails to harness the power of the wind. They were small and cramped, and extremely uncomfortable. Dependent as they were on the wind, they could take months to complete a crossing.

Passengers and crew suffered greatly on these voyages. The Atlantic was a wild, vast ocean. Storms often raged there. Many ships were lost and all on board drowned. Yet despite this, people from all over Europe and Asia were willing to take the risk in order to begin a new life in this exciting new country.

They travelled for numerous reasons. Many were escaping poverty, others were escaping religious persecution. Many were fleeing from wars which seemed to be forever raging in Europe. Whatever the reason, all were hoping for a new, more certain and prosperous life in America.

By the nineteenth century America was a vastly different country to what it had been at the time of Columbus. Cities like New York and Boston were being built. Men had travelled across the vast country from the east to the west coast. Gold had been discovered in California, which led to the famous gold rush of 1849.

In the south, huge plantations grew cotton and tobacco. Slaves, brought on ships across the Atlantic from Africa, supplied the labour. On the vast prairies men had begun to raise cattle and grow grain crops like wheat to feed the population.

The country was rich in iron and coal. Huge smelting works sprung up to supply iron and steel to the construction industry. Men did indeed become rich beyond their wildest dreams in this land of opportunity.

These men built a telegraph line which linked the east and west coasts. Now too they dreamed of building a 3,000 mile long railroad line to cross the whole country. A vast army of workers would be needed to build this railroad and the new towns and cities, which would spring up along the tracks.

As people in Europe learned of these opportunities, they clamoured to travel to America and avail of them.

Those who were willing to travel further west could lay claim to land. Here they could farm the land and raise families.

In Ireland there was great poverty and hardship. To escape from it, many thousands of Irishmen and women decided to seek their fortune in America. But in 1845, an event occurred in Ireland that was to literally drive millions of Irish people to America: the Great Famine.

In 1845 Ireland was ruled by Britain. Landlords owned most of the land. Many of these landlords lived in Britain and agents managed their estates. These agents rented the land to the Irish peasants who eked out a miserable existence on a few acres. Most families lived in mud cabins and depended on the potato for their staple food. Any other crops they produced had to be sold to obtain money to pay their rents.

If a peasant could not pay his rent, he and his family were evicted. With no money, no food and nowhere to live, they were faced with death, or entering the workhouse. One other alternative was to emigrate to Britain or America.

In 1845 the population of Ireland was 8,000,000. The vast majority of those were peasants, depending on the potato for their basic food. If anything were to happen to the crop of potatoes, then a disaster of major proportions would occur.

In 1845 the unthinkable happened. Blight attacked the potatoes, rotting them in the earth. People starved as famine gripped the country. Over the next three years, the famine raged. It was worst in 1847, a year that became known as Black '47.

Faced with starvation and no hope, hundreds of thousands fled the country. Most went to America. Such was the demand for passage to America, that many unscrupulous shipping companies offered passage on ships that were unsuitable for crossing the stormy Atlantic. Many of these ships sank on the journey. All those on board were drowned.

The passengers travelled in the dark holds, which prior to that had been used to transport cargo. Because of the great loss of life on these rotting, leaky ships, they became known as 'coffin ships'.

Conditions on these ships were appalling. For most of the voyage, the passengers were confined to the holds. Here they lived in dark, airless and cramped conditions. They even had to provide and cook their own food.

Toilet facilities were of the most primitive kind and often disease raged among the passengers. The ships were small and easily tossed about on the ocean and seasickness was another factor that made life miserable. When a storm raged, these conditions became even worse.

But so desperate were those passengers to escape the famine and disease raging in Ireland, that they were willing to risk their lives to get to America. Here there were opportunities for work and if they worked, then they would not starve.

By the time of the 1851 census the Irish population had fallen to 6,500,000. Over the coming years it would continue to fall as more and more left, seeking a new and better life. By the turn of the century it was estimated that 4,000,000 Irish people had fled to America.

These later emigrants travelled in much better conditions than those endured by the earlier emigrants. By the end of the century, the era of the sailing ship was at an end. A new era of steam-driven ships had dawned. These were no longer built of wood but of steel. As a consequence they could be much bigger than the old wooden sailing vessels.

With the advent of steam, ships were no longer dependent on the wind, though the earliest steam-driven ships also had sails. Now ships could cross the Atlantic in a much shorter time than the sailing ships. They could also keep to regular schedules because they were no longer so dependent on the weather.

By the end of the nineteenth century, huge steam-driven ocean liners plied the Atlantic route from Europe to America. Some companies, like the Cunard Line, were British. Others, like The Hamburg-Amerika line, were German. One of the most prestigious and famous of all of them was The White Star Line.

By a strange coincidence, in the very first year of the Great Famine, 1845, a man called Henry Threlfall Wilson, with his partner, John Pilkington, founded a shipping company in Liverpool. They named it The White Star Line and their emblem was a white, five-sided star on a red flag.

At first they operated traditional sailing ships and carried cargo and emigrants to Australia. Then, in 1863, they acquired the *Royal Standard*, their first steam ship. The following year it collided with an iceberg on the return journey from Australia.

Was this an omen for the future? It was The White Star Line which would one day own another ship that would also strike an iceberg. This was to be The White Star Line's most famous ship – indeed the most famous ship of all time. She was the *Titanic*.

3

THE WHITE STAR LINE

S hortly after the accident to the *Royal Standard*, The
White Star Line began to have financial difficulties.
Eventually it went bankrupt and a man called Thomas
Henry Ismay bought its name and emblem for £1,000.
Later the name Ismay was to become forever linked
with that of *Titanic*.

Ismay was from Liverpool and was involved in the
shipping industry. In order to raise the £1,000 to buy
the name and emblem of The White Star Line, he
turned to a man called Gustav Schwabe. He was a
Liverpool banker and agreed to lend Ismay the money

on one condition. From then on The White Star Line must have all its ships built in Belfast by the ship-builders, Harland & Wolff.

Schwabe had a personal reason for making this request. His nephew was Gustav Wolff, the partner in the Harland & Wolff shipyard. Wolff was an engineer and had joined the firm of William Harland in 1857 when Schwabe had loaned money to Harland in order to buy out a rival.

This coming together of Ismay, Schwabe and Harland & Wolff around 1860 was to ultimately lead to the building of the *Titanic* 50 years later.

At first The White Star Line concentrated on the Australian routes. But by 1870, the routes from Europe to America were becoming busier. More and more ships were crossing the Atlantic, bringing people from Europe, anxious to find new prospects in this exciting country.

By now too wealthy people from Europe also wanted to visit America. They were also interested in whatever opportunities might be available to increase their wealth.

Those who had by now prospered in America wished to visit Europe. Many of their ancestors had come from that continent and no doubt they wished to see their homelands. They were also anxious to visit famous cities like London, Paris and Rome and to see the great works of art housed in their art galleries.

They also wanted to visit famous holiday destinations like the Cote D'Azur in the south of France. The pyramids of Egypt, the only wonders of the ancient world still in existence, were also a top attraction.

Those who travelled, both from Europe and America, were fabulously wealthy. The only means of travelling across the Atlantic was by ship. Air travel was still a long way off. Being wealthy, they did not wish to travel in the conditions experienced by the earlier pioneers of the Atlantic crossings. They wanted comfort and luxury, and were willing and able to pay for it.

Shipping companies were quick to see these new opportunities. One of those was The White Star Line. They had two ships built at Harland & Wolff in 1871, *Oceanic* and *Atlantic*. Thus The White Star Line's tradition of building ships whose names ended in 'ic' was born.

These ships provided great luxury for wealthy passengers who would travel First Class in cabins on the upper decks. Less luxurious accommodation was also provided below the First Class cabins for those who were less wealthy. This was the Second Class.

However, the vast majority of passengers, like those from Ireland who were going to America seeking work and a new life, would still travel in steerage, that is on the lower decks. This would become known as Third Class.

Nevertheless, these Third Class passengers would still travel in luxury when compared to the conditions endured by those who had fled the famine. They were provided with bunks in cabins they shared with other passengers. No longer did they have to provide or cook their own food. They could now eat in their own dining room and were served by stewards. For many, who had previously not known where their next meal was coming from, this was luxury and privilege indeed.

Under the expertise of Thomas Ismay and a new partner, William Imrie, The White Star Line was soon the undoubted leader in Atlantic travel. But the line also seemed destined to disaster. *Atlantic* was lost when it struck rocks near Nova Scotia in 1873, with the loss of around 550 people. In the following years other ships of The White Star Line were also lost. These disasters were to eventually culminate in the loss of the *Titanic* 39 years after the *Atlantic* disaster.

By the end of the nineteenth century there was great rivalry among shipping companies on the transatlantic route. They vied with each other in terms of the luxury of their ships and speed of crossing. The ship achieving the fastest crossing was awarded the Blue Riband, a highly coveted prize.

Ships of The White Star Line like *Majestic* and *Teutonic* held the Blue Riband in the 1890's. The Cunard

Line, founded in Britain in 1839, also held the Blue Riband on a number of occasions. But by the beginning of the twentieth century, German built ships, notably the *Deutschland*, made the Blue Riband their own.

This was a blow to British pride and Cunard decided to build two liners that not only would be the most luxurious on the Atlantic route but also the fastest. These ships were the *Lusitania* and her sister ship, *Mauretania*.

In 1907 *Lusitania* captured the Blue Riband and held it until 1909. Then the *Mauretania* took the record for the fastest crossing, a record it would hold for twenty years. While these achievements restored British pride and gained much publicity for Cunard, they dealt a severe blow to the prestige of The White Star Line and its new President, Joseph Bruce Ismay.

J.B. Ismay was the son of Thomas Ismay, who had bought The White Star Line in the 1860's. The latter had died in 1899 and his son had taken over the running of the shipping line. Three years later, in 1902, the International Mercantile Marine Company, known as IMM, bought The White Star Line for £10,000,000.

IMM was one of the largest shipping companies in America. It was owned by J. Pierpont Morgan, one of America's richest men. He had interests in banking, steel and railroads, as well as shipping.

Ismay had at first resisted the attempt by IMM to take over his company. But in the end he had to bow to the inevitable. He was a far-seeing man and now he saw a way to restore the prestige of The White Star Line. With the financial backing of J. Pierpont Morgan, he would build the finest ships ever seen. He would leave vulgar matters like speed to others. Instead, his ships would be the largest and most luxurious to ever sail the Atlantic Ocean.

By a strange coincidence, another contemporary also had such a dream. He was Viscount William Pirrie, Chairman of Harland & Wolff. He summoned Ismay to a meeting at his home in London, 1907 and there the two men decided to embark on their dream.

Little did either man know that one of those ships they now proposed to build would become, for reasons neither could ever have foreseen, the most famous ocean liner of all time, the ill-fated *Titanic*.

4

A Dream is Born

On a summer's evening in 1907 a chauffeur-driven limousine pulled up at Downshire House in Belgrave Square, a fashionable area of London. Here the very rich and famous lived in great luxury. The passengers in the limousine were Bruce Ismay and his wife, Florence. They were coming to dinner at the home of Viscount William Pirrie.

William Pirrie was born in Quebec, Canada, in 1847. Two years later, on the death of his father, the family came to live in County Down with William's paternal grandfather. The family were involved in shipping and it was only natural that William would also take an interest in the industry.

He joined Harland & Wolff as an apprentice in 1862 and rapidly gained promotion in the firm. Then, in 1895, Edward Harland died and shortly after, William became chairman of the firm. At this time he was also elected lord mayor of Belfast. In 1898 he was made the First Freeman of Belfast, an honour that was also bestowed on Thomas Ismay, Bruce Ismay's father.

In 1906 William Pirrie was made a peer and held the title Viscount Pirrie. At this time Gustav Wolff had retired from Harland & Wolff and Pirrie acquired Wolff's shares in the company. Now he had total charge of Harland & Wolff and was determined to maintain its reputation as one of the finest shipbuilders in the world.

From the times of Gustav Schwabe, the ships of The White Star Line had been built by Harland & Wolff. William Pirrie not only had shares in the shipping company but was also proud of its achievements, and of the ships Harland & Wolff built for it.

But this pride had been severely dented by the success of Cunard, The White Star Line's great rival. Pirrie, like Bruce Ismay, was anxious to restore the pride of The White Star Line. It was to discuss how this might be done that he had summoned Bruce Ismay to dinner at Downshire House that summer evening.

After dinner the men retired to the smoking room and here the dream to restore the prestige of The White Star Line was set in motion. It is claimed that the plan to build two (a third was later added) magnificent ocean-going liners was Pirrie's. But whether the plan was Pirrie's or Ismay's, the latter was an enthusiastic supporter.

The proposed ships were to be around 45,000-ton luxury liners and would dwarf the 31,550-ton *Lusitania* and *Mauretania*, Cunard's star ships. The new liners were to be known as Olympic Class ships and were to be named, *Olympic*, *Titanic* and *Gigantic*. This latter name was later changed to *Britannic*.

The sheer size of the proposed ships was nothing short of extraordinary. They were to be 290 metres in length, 30 metres in width and the height of a fourteen-storey building. The first two would be built side by side and were to become known as sister ships.

As William Pirrie and Bruce Ismay smoked their cigars and drank their brandy, they had good reason to feel pleased. Harland & Wolff would build these magnificent ships. Bruce Ismay would ensure that they were a success once launched. And IMM, with its unlimited wealth, would fund the venture. A new era on the transatlantic route was about to be born.

One man not present at that meeting, but who was

to play a key part in the whole venture, was Thomas Andrews. He was born in Comber, a village near Belfast, in 1873. His mother, Eliza, was a sister of William Pirrie and so Thomas was Pirrie's nephew.

Thomas Andrews joined Harland & Wolff in 1899 and like his uncle before him, rapidly proved himself an able worker. He was passionately interested in ship design and his designs were regarded as being innovative.

He was granted a seat on the board and by 1907, when Pirrie and Ismay met to discuss their dream, Andrews was managing director of the design department at Harland & Wolff. On his return to Belfast, Pirrie summoned a meeting of what he termed his 'splendid men' at the shipyard. Among them were Alexander Carlisle, Edward Wilding and Thomas Andrews.

It was an exciting and momentous occasion for all present. As they left the meeting, each man held an image in his mind of the great ships they would now build. But while Pirrie and Carlisle could go away and dwell on their dream, there was no such luxury for Thomas Andrews and his deputy, Edward Wilding.

They were the men who would design the ships and now they had months of hard work and dedication ahead of them to bring the dream to fruition. Only then could they stand back for a moment and admire their creations. Then, the pictures they carried in their minds and that they had drawn on paper, would become real in the shape of two magnificent ocean-going liners, the finest ever built.

By the summer of 1908 the designs were ready. Now the building of the ships could commence. An order was formally put forward for the building of two ships, at a cost of £3,000,000. A third would be built later.

16 December 1908 was a momentous day. On this day the keel of the *Olympic* was laid down at the Harland & Wolff shipyard. Just over three months later, on 31 March 1909, a second keel was laid down. This keel was for the *Titanic*, which was to be the largest ship ever built.

5

BUILDING *TITANIC*

With the keel laid, work now continued on building the *Titanic* side by side with her sister ship. No ships of this size had ever been built before and it was important that the structure was immensely strong. This structure consisted of the keel itself, with a steel rib frame attached. To this were riveted the 25mm steel plates which would form the hull.

Safety was a priority and the *Titanic* was fitted with a double bottom. This meant that if she ran aground and the outer plates were holed, the inner ones would prevent water flooding the ship.

Bulkheads, 25mm thick, were built to divide the hull

into sixteen watertight, box-like sections. Each of these fifteen bulkheads had an opening, which could be closed automatically in an emergency. Thus the sixteen watertight compartments in the *Titanic* could be isolated, one from the other, by closing the bulkhead doors. If one compartment was holed in a collision, the water which poured in could be contained in that section. It could not flow throughout the ship.

In fact, the *Titanic* was designed to float even if two of her compartments were flooded. This fact made the ship very safe indeed and led to the myth, which was circulated at the time of her construction and maiden voyage, that she was unsinkable.

A giant ship like the *Titanic*, weighing over 46,000 tons, needed an immense amount of power to drive her propellers. This power was supplied by 29 boilers, which were contained in six boiler rooms. Over 7,000 tons of coal to fire the boilers were held in bunkers on either side of the bulkheads, which separated the boiler rooms.

The boilers produced steam, which in turn was used to power two massive, four-cylinder engines. These each produced an astonishing 15,000 horsepower (hp). This immense power drove two three-bladed propellers cast in bronze and situated on either side of the rudder at the stern. Each propeller measured 8 metres in diameter and weighed a massive 38 tons.

A third four-bladed propeller, five metres in diameter and weighing 22 tons, was situated in the centre of the stern. This was driven by a Parsons turbine, which ran on the waste exhaust steam.

The three engines running at their normal maximum range could produce sufficient power to give the *Titanic* a speed of 21 knots. However, at full power she could reach 23.5 or even 24 knots. This was less than the speed of her Cunard rivals but Ismay and Pirrie were more interested in size, luxury and comfort than speed.

Vertically the ship was divided into ten decks. The lower decks provided room for the engines and boilers and other necessary equipment to operate an ocean-going liner. Here too cargo was carried. Above these decks were the kitchens, dining rooms, lounges and the three classes of passenger accommodation. There was also a post room where mail would be sorted while the liner was crossing the Atlantic.

Many luxuries were provided for the passengers to pass the time during the crossings. There was a swimming pool, a gymnasium, Turkish baths and a squash court. A library was also provided and a hospital area. Some of the most expensive suites in First Class rivalled those of the best hotels in the world for comfort and luxury.

Even the cabins provided for the Third Class passengers had hot and cold running water and electric light.

Truly *Titanic* was the most magnificent ship ever built. No expense was spared in her construction, and even minor details like the number of screws used to fix hooks in the First Class suites troubled Thomas Andrews.

However, one matter in the area of safety was overlooked and that was the capacity of the *Titanic's* lifeboats. This was woefully inadequate, though it complied with regulations at the time. This lack of lifeboat capacity was to become starkly relevant on the night of 15 April 1912 and was to lead to one of the worst tragedies ever to occur at sea.

The *Titanic* was built to carry 2,434 passengers – 708 in First Class, 510 in Second Class and 1,216 in Third Class. She also had a crew of 892. This meant she had a total capacity of 3,326 people. Though there were life-jackets on board for 3,560, the lifeboats could only accommodate 1,178 people.

This lack of lifeboat capacity did not trouble those who attended the launch of the *Titanic* on 31 May 1911, seven months after the launch of her sister ship, the *Olympic*. Wishing to attract maximum publicity for The White Star Line, the *Olympic* sailed from Belfast on the very day that the *Titanic* was launched.

This momentous, sunny day attracted thousands to the Harland & Wolff shipyards. Flags blew in the breeze and there was an air of gaiety and expectation. A number of VIPs watched the launch, including Viscount Pirrie, Bruce Ismay and J. Pierpont Morgan.

The slipway was greased so that the ship could slide smoothly forward on her first short journey. Everything was ready. Unlike the launching of other ships, there was no traditional bottle of champagne smashed against the bow prior to launch.

At around 12.30pm, the *Titanic*, the largest moveable man-made object in the world, began to move. Slowly she slid down the slipway. One minute after starting her journey, she entered the water for the first time.

The launch was not without incident or tragedy. A worker at the shipyard was killed. Previously, during the construction, another worker had also been killed. Perhaps both deaths were omens of what was to happen on the Atlantic on a dark April night less than a year later.

After the launch, the fitting out of the *Titanic* began. This included the fitting of the four massive funnels. Originally the ship was to have three funnels but a fourth, in fact a dummy funnel, was later added to the design.

It was felt that this fourth funnel gave the ship a more pleasing and balanced look. The funnels were also raked backwards slightly, giving the impression of a ship underway at speed, its funnels tilting back in the wind.

At this time the interior of the ship was also completed.

No expense was spared and the magnificence of the First Class accommodation rivalled Louis XVI and Maria Antoinette's famous French palaces at Versailles.

Some of the suites were panelled in wood and had highly decorated moulded ceilings. Furniture here and throughout the ship was stylish and elegant, and had been made by the finest of craftsmen, known for their attention to the smallest details.

The most striking feature on the ship was the main staircase, which led to the First Class lounge. It was 5 metres wide and 20 metres high. It had elegantly carved banisters and elaborate wrought ironwork, and was capped by a magnificent glass dome beneath which hung a glittering chandelier.

The staircase, with its huge dome, was the ultimate symbol of the luxury, power and prestige of the fabulous *Titanic*. But after the tragedy, it was to become a rather different symbol. Now it was seen as a warning to man of how helpless he, and what he might build, could become when faced with the immense power of nature.

In the event that the ship might become a victim of nature's immense power and encounter a calamity at sea, the *Titanic* was also fitted with a device that could prove crucial in any emergency that might arise. This device was a radio transmitter and receiver, and indeed it would play a significant part in the tragedy that was to befall the ship.

Even in 1912, radio was still a relatively new invention. It had been invented by Guglielmo Marconi, who was born in Bologna, in Italy, in 1874. Whilst his father was Italian, his mother was Irish. In 1898 Marconi succeeded in transmitting radio signals in Morse code across the English Channel. Three years later he successfully transmitted signals across the Atlantic. In 1909 he shared the Nobel Prize for physics.

Marconi was not just a brilliant inventor but was also an acute businessman. He immediately saw the immense potential of radio and the possible myriad uses to which it could be put. In order to exploit his invention, he set up the Marconi Telegraph Company in London.

One area in which he envisaged he could put his invention to good use was shipping. With a radio transmitter/receiver on board, ships could communicate with the shore or with other ships while at sea.

This would certainly appeal to the rich and famous passengers carried on the ocean-going liners. They could keep in contact with their families while at sea and just as important, they could keep in contact with their businesses and the stock markets.

But where this invention could really be worth its weight in gold would be in the event of an emergency at sea. In such a situation, a ship could send out a distress message to other ships or to shore-based rescue stations.

Before the advent of radio, the only way a ship could contact another ship was with the use of flags, by signal light, or with flares. With the former two methods, the ships had to be in visual contact with each other. Flares, on the other hand, when fired high in the air could be seen from a long way off. But none of these methods could match the capabilities of direct radio contact.

This fact had been most clearly demonstrated on 23 January 1909. During thick fog, a collision occurred off Nantucket on America's east coast between The White Star Line's ship, the *Republic* and an Italian ship, the *Florida*.

The *Republic*, under Captain Sealby, was sailing between Boston and Liverpool with 500 people on board. The *Florida* was sailing from Naples to New York with 343 passengers on board.

Despite the seriousness of the collision and the large number of passengers and crew on both ships, there were only five fatalities in all. This was due to the fact that Captain Ruspini of the *Florida* was able to send out a distress call for assistance on his radio.

Jack Bins was the radio operator on duty that day and he became a hero in America. His repeated distress call was picked up by The White Star Line's ship, the *Baltic*, which quickly arrived in the area. By then, the *Republic* was almost engulfed by water and there was terrible panic on board. But despite the radio room being flooded, Bins stuck to his task until he summoned help.

The *Baltic* successfully completed the rescue of the panicking passengers and took them to New York. The *Republic*, however, was severely damaged and sank. If it had not been for the arrival of the *Baltic*, many more lives would have been lost.

So the *Titanic*, where no expense had been spared in her construction or fitting out, naturally had its own radio room, situated aft of the bridge. Here was kept the radio transmitter/receiver. It had its own steam-driven electric generator and as an extra precaution still, it also had a back-up power supply in the form of batteries.

With the fitting out completed, it seemed that at last the *Titanic* was ready to take on its rivals in the shipping world. Once its sea trials were completed and the ship was passed as fit to sail, the *Titanic* could undertake its maiden crossing of the Atlantic.

This was originally scheduled for 20 March 1912. But in September 1911, the *Olympic* sustained damage in a collision with the cruiser, HMS *Hawke*, and had to return to Belfast for repairs. Work temporarily ceased on the *Titanic* as those involved in her fitting out now recommenced work on the *Olympic*.

In the collision, the *Olympic* had sustained damage

to two of her watertight compartments. But despite the fact that both compartments were flooded, she had been able to return safely to Southampton. This fact seemed to amply prove the claim that the two sister ships were, in fact, unsinkable.

The date for the *Titanic*'s maiden voyage was rescheduled for 10 April 1912. Now with the myth that she was unsinkable reinforced by the experience of the *Olympic*, it seemed as if the *Titanic* was invincible.

No one could have foreseen that on that maiden voyage, she was destined to encounter an iceberg, which weeks earlier had broken off from the great northern icecap. Even as the *Titanic* was setting sail, the iceberg was slowly but surely floating south into the cold, dark waters of the Atlantic Ocean. By a stroke of chance, the invincible *Titanic* was destined to strike this iceberg and in less than three hours sink beneath the Atlantic Ocean.

6

TITANIC SETS SAIL

Monday 1 April 1912, April Fools' Day, was the day set for the *Titanic*'s sea trials. However, due to adverse weather these were postponed until the following day. So it was on Tuesday 2 April that the *Titanic* took to the open seas for the first time.

After being towed out from her berth, she then proceeded out to sea under her own power. All that day she underwent many trials to ensure that she was seaworthy. Her engines and steering were checked, as was all her other essential equipment. It was found that from a speed of 20 knots she could stop in a little less than 300 metres, a very impressive achievement for such a large ship.

Her response to the rudder was less impressive but still regarded as adequate. However, no one could have foreseen that this lack of response would prove fatal on the night of 15 April, an unlucky thirteen days from then.

Thomas Andrews and Edward Wilding were on board to oversee the trials. Also on board was Francis Carruthers. He was the representative from the Board of Trade and the man ultimately responsible for granting the ship its certificate of seaworthiness. This document gave the *Titanic* permission to carry paying passengers.

The trials were deemed successful and Carruthers signed the certificate. The *Titanic* returned to Belfast and prepared to sail for the port of Southampton on the south coast of England.

At 8pm on 2 April the *Titanic* left Belfast for the first time. She was destined never to return to the place of her birth.

She arrived in Southampton late the next day and was towed into her berth at The White Star Dock. Here she would take on her full complement of crew and her first passengers. Then, under the command of Captain Edward John Smith, she would sail for Cherbourg in France.

Smith was the senior captain of The White Star Line and was captain of the *Olympic*. Now, as befitting his senior position, he was given command of the line's most prestigious ship. Smith was due to retire at the end of the voyage and sailing the magnificent *Titanic* into New York would be a fitting end to his career.

For some unknown reason, Smith requested that Henry Tingle Wilde, chief officer of the *Olympic*, be transferred to the *Titanic* as its chief officer. This request was granted and Chief Officer William McMaster Murdoch was demoted to first officer to accommodate Wilde. First Officer Charles Herbert Lightoller was then demoted to second officer.

There was no direct evidence ever presented that this caused resentment or contributed to the later tragedy. But it is likely that there was some resentment and confusion at this change of personnel at such short notice. It certainly was not an ideal situation to prevail, especially during an emergency.

In fact, there was already a problem on the ship. A fire had broken out in Number 10 bunker, adjacent to boiler room Number 6. This was not an unusual occurrence on a ship but afterwards there was much speculation as to whether the fire had weakened the bulkhead, which collapsed so dramatically on the night of the collision. Certainly the collapse of the bulkhead meant that the ship sank a little sooner.

In the weeks leading up to the *Titanic*'s maiden voyage, there had been a coal miner's strike in Britain. Because of the lack of coal, ships could not sail and many were berthed at Southampton.

The strike was settled on 6 April, four days before the *Titanic* sailed. But because passengers were reluctant to book a passage while the strike was on, the liner left Southampton with just over 900 passengers on board and a crew of 892. Had there not been a strike it is certain that the ship would have sailed with a full complement of passengers and the loss of life in the tragedy would have been far worse.

At noon on 10 April, the *Titanic* cast off and sailed from Southampton for Cherbourg in France. On the way out of the harbour, the suction her passage created caused the liner *New York* to break her mooring ropes.

She swung out into the path of the massive *Titanic* and a collision seemed inevitable. It was simply prevented by the quick action of a tugboat, which nudged the *New York* out of the way. At the same time the crew on the *Titanic* took evasive action and put her engines full astern to slow the ship down.

It was not the start that anyone might have wished for. Mrs Harris, an American passenger who witnessed the incident, was asked by a male passenger if she enjoyed life. When she answered that she did, he told her that the *Titanic* was an unlucky ship and advised her to disembark at Cherbourg.

She did not heed the man's advice and remained

onboard. But while the ship's luck ran out, Mrs Harris did survive the sinking, though it is not known what happened to the passenger who had spoken to her.

After a delay of about an hour, the *Titanic* continued on her journey to Cherbourg where she picked up more passengers while others, not knowing how lucky they were, disembarked. At 8pm she sailed once more, this time for Cobh, then known as Queenstown, a port on the south coast of Ireland.

The *Titanic* anchored off shore at Queenstown at 11.30am on Thursday 11 April. Two tenders, *America* and *Ireland*, ferried passengers and mail out to the ship. Seven passengers disembarked here. One of them was Frances Browne who was destined to become famous as Father Browne, who had photographed the ship.

One other to leave the ship at Queenstown was John Coffey, a stoker. He actually deserted his post, though it is not known why. Since he lived in the area, perhaps he had availed of a free trip home.

Two hours after dropping anchor, the *Titanic* was underway again, bound for New York. As she sailed away from the coast of Ireland, a lone piper played a tune, 'Erin's Lament', on the Third Class Promenade deck. This man was Eugene Daly.

Like Daniel Buckley, a young man from Kingswilliamstown (now called Ballydesmond), County

Cork, and many of those passengers travelling in Third Class, Daly was emigrating to America to start a new life for himself. And, like many of his fellow Third Class passengers, he never expected to return to Ireland.

What none of the passengers could have known was that most of them would never reach America. Within four days they would lie far beneath the Atlantic Ocean, the ship they now sailed on destined to be their final resting place.

But none of those thoughts were in the passengers' minds right then, whether they were in Third Class or Second Class, or the more illustrious ones travelling First Class. Here, in the finest suites and cabins on the ship, were some of the wealthiest and most important men and woman in the world at that time.

Couples like Colonel John Jacob Astor and his wife Madeleine; or Isidor and Ida Straus who co-owned Macy's, the most famous store in New York; or Sir Cosmo and Lady Duff-Gordon who were travelling under the assumed name of Morgan.

J. Pierpont Morgan was due to travel on *Titanic's* maiden voyage but was advised against it on health grounds. Did the Duff-Gordon's, who were notorious publicity seekers, take the name Morgan so as to appear part of the Morgan family, then one of the richest in the world, and impress other passengers? It is a question that, like so many others about the *Titanic* and those who sailed on her, will never be answered.

Others on board were Benjamin Guggenheim, a wealthy American, and Major Archibald Willingham Butt, a personal aide to the American president. Colonel Archibald Gracie was yet another distinguished American on the ship. American Margaret Brown, was also aboard, later to be immortalised as 'The Unsinkable Molly Brown'.

In Second Class were the Becker family, including twelve-year-old Ruth who would behave with great generosity on the night of the sinking. Also in Second Class was a man and two children travelling, like the Duff-Gordon's, under an assumed name. After the sinking, the children were to become famous because their father had snatched them from their mother.

Also on board for the maiden voyage were Bruce Ismay and Thomas Andrews. They were anxious to see how the ship performed and Andrews spent a great deal of his time checking out every detail that required attention.

Those first days at sea were uneventful. There were no major problems and the *Titanic* performed perfectly. The weather was cold, despite it being bright and sunny. The cold kept most passengers indoors where they enjoyed the experience of being at sea on the finest ship ever to set sail.

To amuse themselves and pass the time they played cards or read or simply sat around and chatted with their fellow passengers. Some availed of the facilities on board like the swimming pool, squash court and gymnasium. The less energetic relaxed with a steam bath or a massage.

Some did face the cold and went for strolls on the decks. A few braver souls took part in the deck games, which were available. Others attended concerts or in Third Class organised their own dances.

Meanwhile, the crew worked hard to ensure that all passengers had a pleasant voyage. Meals were served to all on board and in First Class no effort was spared in catering to every whim of the rich and famous. Here too they could relax to the strains of the ship's orchestra.

Two of those on board were extremely busy during this time. They were the radio operators, Jack Phillips and Harold Bride. They were employed not by The White Star Line but by the Marconi Company that provided and operated the radio on ships at that time.

Both men were even busier than usual because the radio transmitter broke down just before midnight on Friday 12 April. They reported the matter to Captain Smith who ordered them to work together to solve the problem. Radio operation was essential and it was important that it got working again very quickly.

Phillips and Bride, who were also radio technicians, worked through the night to isolate and repair the fault. It proved a difficult problem and it was morning before they discovered that the breakdown had been caused by a short circuit in the wiring.

But by Saturday morning they were able to report to the bridge that normal radio transmission could resume. And although both men were tired, they now had to continue their shifts and deal with a backlog of messages.

As well as sending messages from the passengers and receiving messages on their behalf, radio was also essential for receiving any warnings of danger, especially that of icebergs on the shipping routes. Normally ships sailed well south of the area where icebergs might be encountered and they did not usually pose a problem.

But the winter of 1911 had been mild and this caused icebergs to float further south than usual. In fact, before the *Titanic* sailed from Southampton there had been reports of icebergs and of one ship, the *Niagara*, being damaged in a collision.

In the days leading up to the disaster there had been at least a dozen if not more reports of icebergs being spotted on the *Titanic*'s planned route. Many of these warnings did reach Captain Smith so he was aware of the dangers that might lie ahead. But despite this, he did not order a reduction in speed or course alteration so as to take the *Titanic* further south and away from the danger.

Among the messages reaching the ship on Sunday 14 April were many that warned of icebergs. One from the *Rappahannock* at 10.30pm was sent by signal lamp, which meant that both ships were in close proximity at the time. The *Rappahannock* had encountered an ice-field so it was obvious that the *Titanic* was also in the vicinity of the ice-field. But despite the warning, no precautions were taken.

Around 11pm, Evans, the radio operator on the *Californian*, contacted the *Titanic* to warn them that his ship was in the middle of an ice-field and had stopped for the night. Jack Phillips was manning the radio. He was still tired from the sleepless night and had been kept extremely busy during his shift.

Phillips became angry with Evans, and told him that he had many messages yet to send and to shut up and leave them be. Evans, obviously upset at this reaction, shut down his transmitter and prepared to retire for the night. He was the sole radio operator on the *Californian*, and a round the clock radio service was not maintained.

Another ship to contact the *Titanic* that evening was the SS *Baltic*, which was carrying the Kerry football team to New York, where they were to go on tour.

On the *Titanic*, Phillips continued transmitting his messages. He wanted to clear the backlog before Harold Bride took over the next shift. On the *Californian*, the radio was silent. Evans had retired to his bunk and would not be woken until early the next morning.

Meanwhile, the *Titanic* sailed on at 22.5 knots, her destiny now decided. She had less than an hour before her encounter with the iceberg. In a little over three hours more the dark Atlantic waters would close over her forever.

7

ICEBERG. DEAD AHEAD!

The night of Sunday 14 April 1912 was dark. There was no moon but the sky was sprinkled with stars. The surface of the Atlantic Ocean was as smooth and black as slate. Only the passage of the liner, *Titanic*, disturbed the surface.

The bow of the ship cut through the ocean like a giant knife blade. On either side the water curled over like earth before a plough. At the stern, the three massive propellers spun at 75 revolutions per second.

Their blades cut through the water, pushing the ship onwards towards New York at 21.5 knots. In the ship's wake, the churned water foamed and seethed. It stretched back into the darkness like a giant white V drawn with chalk on a blackboard.

The time was 11.40pm. High up in the crow's nest on the foremast, two sailors were on lookout duty. At this time, neither sonar (which can detect objects under the water) nor radar (which can detect objects above the water) had been invented. So human lookouts provided the eyes and ears of the ships that sailed the oceans of the world.

The *Titanic's* lookouts, Frederick Fleet and Reginald Lee, had taken up their watch at 10pm that night. They were well wrapped up, as the crow's nest was exposed to the elements. But, despite their protective clothing, they were bitterly cold.

The air temperature stood at freezing point while the temperature of the water was still lower. There was no wind to moan through the rigging but the ship's momentum was sufficient to create an artificial breeze. It numbed the exposed faces of the lookouts and stung their eyes, making them water.

Though ordinary seamen, that night they were probably the most important men on the ship, scanning the ocean ahead for danger. And they knew that great danger lurked out there in the darkness. It was a danger that all seamen sailing this far north on the Atlantic Ocean feared. That danger was ice.

On this voyage the danger was very real. Through the previous Saturday there had been many reports of sightings of ice. Throughout that day, the *Titanic* had also received warnings of ice ahead.

One message, sent by radio from Captain Barr of the *Caronia*, had warned of icebergs, growlers and field ice lying right in the path of the liner. This report was regarded as being so serious that it was posted on the bridge where the captain and officers could see it. The more serious report from the cargo ship, the S.S. *Rappahannock*, was received by signal lamp only half an hour after Fleet and Lee took over lookout duty.

But despite these serious warnings of danger, no action was taken to prevent a possible collision. The ship's speed was not reduced. No order was given to alter course so as to take the ship further south and away from potential hazards.

Captain Smith, after dining with a group of passengers in the First Class Dining Room, had retired to his cabin at 9.20pm. This clearly was not the behaviour of a man who thought his ship might be in grave danger.

Was this ignoring of potential danger due to the fact that the *Titanic* was thought of as unsinkable? Did the sheer size and magnificence of the ship, at that time the largest movable man-made object in the world, add to this aura of invincibility which seemed to hang about her? Who can ever know now? But it seems possible, as the IMM Group issued a statement after first reports of the sinking to the effect that the ship could withstand any damage and could not have sunk.

What seems probable is that the ship's speed was not reduced or its course altered for two reasons. One was due to an attempt, at the behest of Bruce Ismay, to run the ship at maximum speed the next day. The *Olympic* had already achieved a speed of nearly 23 knots and it seems that Ismay wanted the *Titanic* to beat this. It would create good publicity for The White Star Line.

It is known that a warning of the presence of ice was seen by Ismay earlier on that fateful Sunday evening. But he kept this warning to himself for several hours. Was this because he feared that it would prevent the attempt at the high-speed run the following day? At the inquiry, he denied knowledge of the ice warnings but from other evidence it is certain that he was aware of the presence of ice.

The second probable reason for the failure to reduce speed was so that the *Titanic* could sail into New York as dawn was just breaking on Wednesday morning. This was the ship's maiden voyage, the dawn of a new era in luxurious transatlantic travel, and perhaps Ismay wanted to use the symbolism of the real dawn to coincide with it.

Whatever the reasons might have been, it was fool-hardy if not downright irresponsible to run the ship at high speed in such circumstances. Why an experienced skipper like Captain Smith did so will forever remain a mystery.

Contrary to reports at the time, the *Titanic* was not making an attempt on the Blue Riband. At this time it was held by the Cunard liner, *Mauretania*, which took the record in 1909 with a maximum speed of 27 knots. Even with all its boilers lit, the *Titanic* could never have achieved anything near such a speed.

It is doubtful if any of these matters were troubling Fleet or Lee in the crow's nest. What would have been troubling them was trying to stay warm in the bitter cold. And another factor which would have been troubling them was the fact that they did not have binoculars.

Though the night was dark, it is possible that with a powerful set of binoculars the iceberg might have been seen earlier and warnings issued in time to avoid a collision. But there were no binoculars on board. They had disappeared before the ship left Southampton. Like many other mysteries concerning the *Titanic*, what happened to the binoculars is yet another that remains unsolved.

With their naked eyes, Fleet and Lee strained to see if any danger lay ahead in that shrouding darkness. Their senses were highly stretched, the enormity of the responsibility weighing heavily on their shoulders.

Meanwhile, the liner, with all its lights blazing like a miniature moving city, sailed on into the night. In his cabin, Captain Smith slept, oblivious to the danger and the tragedy that was about to befall his command.

Most of the passengers were in their beds, dreaming of sailing into New York on Wednesday morning and for many of them, having their first glimpse of the Statue of Liberty and the skyscrapers of Manhattan standing like tall fingers pointing to the sky. Other passengers sat in the lounges or smoking rooms, playing cards or having a final drink before retiring for the night.

Around 11.30pm the lookouts noticed a slight haze or fog dead ahead. It could signify that there was ice in the vicinity. They discussed warning those on the bridge but decided not to. Instead, they became even more alert and peered into the darkness with greater intensity.

The minutes passed. The *Titanic* sailed on majestically. Then at 11.40pm Frederick Fleet spotted a vague, grey shape looming ahead out of the darkness. For a moment he stared intently with his stinging eyes, a tremor of fear coursing through his body. Then, without waiting for confirmation from Lee, he sprang into action.

He grabbed the cord of the warning bell in the crow's nest and tugged it sharply three times. The peals of the brass bell rang out stark and clear in the still night. It warned those on the bridge of the imminent danger of a stationary object right ahead. Almost in the same instant, Fleet grabbed the telephone and rang through to the bridge.

Sixth Officer Moody was on the bridge and had already heard the warning bell. So when he answered the telephone, he knew that he was about to hear the words he and many others had been secretly dreading: Iceberg! Dead ahead!

Despite what must have been a terrible shock, Officer Moody, as befitting a well-trained and experienced ship's officer, thanked Fleet for the information. Staying remarkably calm in the circumstances, he then informed First Officer Murdoch that an iceberg lay ahead directly in the path of *Titanic*.

Murdoch, in the absence of the captain, was in command of the ship. To his credit, he immediately sprang into action. He ordered the helmsman, Quartermaster Robert Hitchens, to go hard-a-starboard. Hitchens immediately obeyed the order, frantically spinning the wheel until it could go no further.

Murdoch then rang down to the engine room on the ship's telegraph the order to stop. This was followed by the order: Full astern. Down below in the bowels of the ship both orders were promptly obeyed. The three propellers ceased to revolve and then began to spin in reverse, biting into the water in a desperate attempt to slow the ship's speed.

On the bridge, Murdoch now sounded the bell that warned everyone below decks that the watertight doors were about to be closed. He then operated the switch, which activated the automatic closing mechanism. The doors closed, sealing off the watertight sections, which were designed to prevent water flowing from one compartment into another.

Like a great iron sea beast, the *Titanic* responded to the reverse thrust of the propellers and imperceptibly began to slow. But without any other means of braking, the effect on the ship's forward momentum, though quite exceptional, was woefully inadequate in the circumstances.

The great ship also responded to the spinning wheel. It controlled the rudder that steered the ship through the water. But to get a ship as large as *Titanic* to change direction takes time.

In the Belfast trials it had been noted that the *Titanic* took an exceptionally long time to respond to the rudder. Now, after an agonising delay of 30 seconds or so, she began to swing to port. She turned, as ships then did, in the opposite direction to the wheel's movement.

On the bridge, Murdoch, Moody and Hitchens could do no more. Ahead lay the huge dark mass of the iceberg. It resembled a great irregular shaped lump of icing on the surface of a vast dark cake. The three men held their breath as the ship swung to port. But was this course alteration too little and was it much too late? If it was, then nothing now could prevent a collision with the iceberg.

Up in the crow's nest, Fleet and Lee could only look on helplessly. Ahead, the iceberg now loomed clearly in the darkness. The lookouts were aware that what was visible was only a tiny fraction of the iceberg towards which the ship was still moving. While above the surface it towered some 60 metres in the air, some 400 or so metres lay hidden beneath the surface of the mirror-smooth ocean.

The lookouts still trembled but it was no longer from the intense cold. They, more than anyone else on the ship, were aware of what was about to happen. They knew that the ship was still travelling much too fast. And though the bow was now swinging away under the influence of the rudder, thus avoiding hitting the iceberg head on, a collision was inevitable.

About 40 seconds after the first peals of the warning bell rang out, the *Titanic* struck the iceberg. The bow had swung away and so the collision was not head on. Had it been, many of the crew and the Third Class passengers in the bow section would have been killed in the impact. But the ship would probably not have sunk.

But because the bow had swung away, it was the starboard side of the ship that came into contact with the iceberg. As the ship sailed on, its side scraped relentlessly against an underwater spar jutting out of the iceberg. This tore a gash in the 25mm thick plates that formed the hull.

The gash was about 100 metres in length. It ran along the sides of the first four watertight compartments and boiler room Number 6. In some places the tear was no wider than the width of a few fingers. In other places it was the width of a hand. In a few places the gash was much larger. It was below the water line, about 3 metres above the keel.

Immediately, water began to pour into the damaged compartments and into boiler room Number 6 at a rate of 8,000 litres per minute. Nothing could stop that relentless gushing water. From that moment, the fate of the *Titanic*, along with that of most of her passengers and crew, was sealed.

8

TITANIC IN PERIL

The *Titanic* juddered under the impact of the collision, which was felt in varying degrees throughout the vessel. Many of those in the bow of the ship were awakened by the impact. Others heard a grating noise, as the hull was ripped open by a jutting spar of the iceberg.

Further back, towards the stern, the impact was hardly noticed. Some stokers, on hearing the noise, thought that the ship had shed a propeller. A stewardess merely noticed a tray of glasses clinking. Many passengers slept on peacefully, oblivious to what had occurred. Even those who were aware could not have imagined the consequences of this seemingly slight impact.

One of those awakened by the alarms, impact and noise was Captain Smith. He immediately came up onto the bridge. He could not have known that his ship was mortally damaged but he was filled with foreboding.

'What has happened?' Smith asked Murdoch.

'We've struck an iceberg,' Murdoch replied, and went on to explain what evasive action he had taken.

Smith and Murdoch now went out on deck to take a look. Aft of the ship, they caught a glimpse of the massive iceberg, once more a vague grey shape in the darkness. Both men must have realised that the collision could have caused serious damage to the ship's hull.

Smith returned to the bridge and rang down to the engine room with the order: Stop. As the engineers complied with the order, the *Titanic's* propellers stopped spinning for the last time. The ship began to slow down. Eventually it stopped and an eerie silence enveloped it.

Fourth Officer Boxhall now arrived on the bridge. He was due to take over the next watch. Smith ordered him to carry out a visual inspection of the damage to the hull. Boxhall went below to check on the forward compartments.

At first there appeared to be no damage. He then met the ship's carpenter who told him that she was taking in water. Another report came from the post office. It was flooded and the workers were trying to rescue the mail-bags, which were floating on a metre or so of water.

Boxhall returned to the bridge and made his report. Captain Smith listened with growing apprehension, the realisation dawning on him that the situation was extremely serious. But even so he could surely not have imagined that his ship could sink.

Though no doubt aware of that possibility, and of the fact that distress messages might need to be sent by wireless, he ordered Boxhall to calculate the *Titanic's* exact position. Boxhall did so and found that the ship was stopped at 41.46N and 50.14W.

This calculation of the ship's position was incorrect by a number of miles. But in the circumstances Boxhall could be excused his error. He was working quickly and under great pressure. Yet, like many other aspects of the *Titanic* story, it is one that has led to much spec-ulation over the years.

Bruce Ismay now arrived on the bridge along with most of the ship's other officers. Ismay wanted to know the seriousness of the situation.

'It seems very serious,' Smith explained, reporting what he knew so far. 'I am now going to carry out an inspection myself. Then we will know the full extent of the damage.'

Captain Smith knew that swift action was vitally

important. But he needed to know for certain what action needed to be taken. Was his ship doomed to sink and would his passengers and crew have to abandon the vessel? If it was necessary to abandon the vessel, then every second counted.

Smith knew that there was one man on board who probably knew more about the *Titanic* than any other man on earth. This man was the ship's designer Thomas Andrews. Smith ordered Andrews to be summoned to the bridge where Andrews was informed of what had occurred.

When Andrews heard the report he realised immediately that the situation was extremely serious. There was a great possibility that the ship would sink. But he reserved his opinion until he, Captain Smith and Chief Officer Wilde went below to make an inspection of the damage.

Andrews realised how perilous the situation was straight away. Number 6 boiler room was already flooding. Four of the forward watertight compartments were also holed and flooding. Two decks below, the post room was under water as was the squash court.

Already, tons of water had entered the bow of the ship. With every passing minute many more tons of water would flood in. The weight would slowly but surely push the bow of the ship deeper and deeper into the sea.

When that happened and the forward compartments

filled, water would lap over the top of the bulkhead in Number 6 boiler room and begin to fill boiler room Number 5. This would add even more weight and force the bow deeper still. Eventually Number 5 boiler room would flood and water from there would then begin to flow into the next compartment.

One by one the other compartments would flood, forcing the ship further into the ocean. Nothing could stop this process. Eventually, under the weight of thousands of tons of water, the *Titanic* would lose her buoyancy and sink to the bottom of the ocean.

The *Titanic* had been built to survive damage to any two of her watertight compartments. Even with three flooded she might have been able to stay afloat. But with five compartments flooded, there was no hope that she could survive.

It was the actions taken by First Officer Murdoch to avoid a collision with the iceberg that now tolled the death knell of the *Titanic*. However, no blame could be attributed to him. He had simply done what any other ship's officer would have done in the circumstances.

After carrying out their inspection and surveying the damage, Captain Smith turned to Andrews and asked the inevitable question: 'Is *Titanic* going to sink?'

'Yes,' Andrews answered. 'The ship will sink.'

'How long have we got?' Smith asked, only too well

aware that every extra minute might mean a life saved.

'One and a half hours,' Andrews replied. 'Perhaps two hours at most. What is certain is that the *Titanic* is doomed.'

The two men stared at each other, each aware of one terrible fact. The ship carried 2,208 people. However, the lifeboats on board could only take 1,178 people. If another ship did not reach the disaster scene to help evacuate the passengers and crew, then at least 1,000 people would die this night in the dark and bitterly cold waters of the Atlantic Ocean.

Aware of this stark fact, Smith, Andrews and Wilde hurried back to the bridge. Here, Smith took the position of the ship, as calculated by Boxhall, and went immediately to the radio room.

'We have struck an iceberg,' Smith told the two radio operators. 'You must start sending the following distress message. "Have hit an iceberg. *Titanic* in great danger. Our position is 41.46N, 50.14W."'

Radio operator Jack Phillips began to transmit the message. First he tapped out the letters MGY, which was the ship's call sign. The letters CQD, which was the recognised sign for a ship in distress, came next. This was then followed by the captain's message.

Many people think that the letters C.Q.D. stand for 'Come quick! Danger!' But in fact they do not mean any such thing. They were simply chosen because they were easy to send in Morse code. Phillips went on sending out the distress message, something he would continually do over the next two hours or so.

Back on the bridge Captain Smith ordered that the crew be mustered and the lifeboats prepared for launching. Stewards were to inform the passengers that they were to put on their life-jackets and assemble on the boat deck. The stewards must do this calmly. They must not alarm the passengers. The last thing Captain Smith wanted on his sinking ship was 2,208 panicking passengers and crew who would gradually become aware that only half of them could be saved.

The captain now stared out into the darkness, seeking any evidence of the presence of another ship. But there was none. His only hope of contacting another ship and summoning it to the rescue now rested with the radio distress calls. Hopefully they would be picked up by a nearby vessel, which would then come to their assistance.

If a ship did come then all his passengers and crew might yet be saved. But if no one came to their assistance, then a great many would die and the ocean bed would become their watery grave.

9

CALLS FOR HELP

As yet there was no sign of panic on board the ship.
Many passengers still slept on, blissfully unaware
of the drama being played out on board and the terrible
danger they were now facing.

Because the First Class passengers were closer to the
open decks, some of those ventured outside to see what
had happened. Many were still in their nightclothes and
seeing that there appeared to be no danger, returned to
the warmth of their beds.

At this stage most of the crew were unaware of the
danger. When passengers inquired about what had
happened they were told that there had been a minor

collision but everything was fine. The ship would soon be underway again.

The passengers readily accepted this explanation. After all, there was no sign of danger or panic. All was calm. And it seemed inconceivable that the 'unsinkable' *Titanic* could sink.

One First Class passenger who had been woken by the collision was Colonel Archibald Gracie. He also became aware that the engines were silent and that the ship had stopped. He got dressed and went up on deck to inspect the ship. There appeared to be no damage but when a fellow passenger handed him a lump of ice, Gracie realised what had happened.

He was a soldier and undoubtedly an astute man. From a description of the iceberg, he realised it was gigantic. If the ship had collided with something that was larger than its self then it was likely that it had sustained serious damage. Gracie decided to remain on deck and await developments.

In the Second Class lounge a group of men were playing cards. They felt the impact and noted that the ship had altered course and then stopped. A steward was sent to investigate and returned to inform them of the collision. When he told them that there was ice on the decks, they laughed and said it could be put in their drinks.

What the steward was referring to was the chunks of

ice from the iceberg, which had fallen onto the decks. At the stern, passengers began to kick the chunks around and some were thrown into cabins through open windows. Even here there was little awareness of what had really happened and the presence of the ice was treated as an opportunity for some horseplay.

Another Second Class passenger, Reverand Thomas Byles, was reading his Bible on the boat deck. Despite the bitter cold, he was enjoying the calm, starry night. He too felt the collision but thought little of it and when he had finished his reading, retired to his cabin.

However, down in the Third Class cabins, at the ship's bow, things were rather different. Here the impact was strongly felt. The grating sound as the hull was torn open wakened many of the sleeping passengers. One passenger who both heard and felt the impact was Daniel Buckley, the young man from County Cork.

He decided to investigate. When he swung his legs out of his bunk, he found himself standing in a pool of water. He knew that the ship was holed and he informed those other passengers who shared his cabin that they might be in grave danger. They laughed at him and told him to go back to sleep. But he was sufficiently perturbed to make the decision to get dressed and go up on deck to see what was happening.

In the engine room, the crew had felt the impact as

little more than a jolt. They knew something was wrong though when the order to stop and go astern was given. But in boiler room Number 6 there could be no doubt about the seriousness of the situation. As water poured in through the gash in the hull, the bulkhead door was closed. Many of the firemen and stokers working in the boiler room scrambled up the escape ladders and barely escaped with their lives.

The ship's second engineer, James Hesketh, reacted quickly to the emergency. He ordered that the pumps be switched on to try and pump out the water entering the ship. Then he ordered the fires to be damped down. As the ship had been travelling at near maximum speed, the steam which drove the turbines was almost at full pressure. He was aware of the possibility of a catastrophic explosion if that pressure was not reduced immediately.

Water was pumped into the fireboxes to quench the fires. This caused steam to billow out, along with ashes. The working conditions for the stokers and firemen were appalling. It was suffocating, extremely hot and breathing was difficult. But due to heroic work, the fires were damped down, thus averting one possible danger.

Rumours now began to circulate among the firemen and stokers further back towards the stern that the forward compartments and cabins were flooding. But at first this was treated as a joke. There could be no danger to the 'unsinkable' *Titanic* from such a slight impact. Indeed in many parts of the ship, like the kitchens, bakeries and laundry, work went on as usual. Here no one had sensed any real threat of danger.

One thing that added to this air of calm was that the electricity did not fail. Lights still burned throughout the ship. The four electric generators, each capable of generating 400 kilowatts of electrical power, were situated above the water line and continued to function. They were steam driven and engineers and firemen and stokers heroically kept up a sufficient amount of steam throughout the next two hours to keep them operating.

They were vital in the emergency. Not only did they keep the lamps lighting but they were also required to operate pumps, winches and many of the safety systems on the ship, including opening and closing the watertight bulkhead doors.

But the most important generator now on the ship was the one supplying power for the radio transmitter. It was vital that steam be supplied to operate this. It did have back-up batteries for emergencies but having normal operating power meant that the operators had one less problem to worry about. Instead, they could concentrate on the most important task in hand – that of summoning help.

In the wireless room, Phillips tapped out the emergency call sign, CQD, over and over again. On his earphones he listened as best he could for a reply. It was difficult to hear as the roar of the excess steam venting from the safety release valves on the pipes attached to the nearby funnel drowned out almost all other sound.

Phillips had asked Captain Smith on one occasion to shut off the safety valves. But Smith, who himself was only too well aware of the problem, could not comply with this request. If the safety valves were closed there was the danger of steam building up and a boiler exploding.

Resigned to the situation, Phillips remained at his post. Three-quarters of an hour had passed since the ship had struck the iceberg. As yet there was no hope of assistance from any other vessel. Unless that assistance soon came, half of those on board the ship were still destined to perish.

10

ABANDON SHIP!

U nknown to Phillips or anyone else on the *Titanic* at that time, there was a ship close by. This was the *Californian*, whose radio operator, Evans, had sent warnings of ice earlier that night. Rebuffed by an angry Jack Phillips, Evans had switched off his radio and retired for the night.

Now, as the *Titanic's* distress call, CQD went out over the airwaves, the one ship close enough to come to the stricken liner's aid, could not hear the latest terrible message: 'We have struck iceberg. Sinking fast. Come to our assistance.'

The *Californian* had earlier encountered an ice field

and Captain Stanley Lord had ordered the ship to stop for the night. On the bridge, Third Officer Charles Groves was on watch. He had tried to signal with his Aldis lamp to a ship that had passed on their port side. But the ship had not responded.

When Captain Lord came onto the bridge around midnight, both men discussed the presence of the ship whose lights they could just see. Second Officer Herbert Stone, who was due to take over the watch, joined the two men on the bridge. He judged that the ship, which appeared to be stationary, was about five miles distant.

But if the ship was the *Titanic* then Stone's estimation of the distance between it and the *Californian* was incorrect. Later estimates put the distance between the two ships as being between 10 and 20 miles.

Captain Lord ordered Stone to inform him if he noticed anything unusual about the other ship. Then Lord retired to his cabin, unaware of the tragedy which was now taking place just a few miles away. If he had only known and acted, many of those who died that night could have been saved.

So, while the *Californian* maintained radio silence, other ships began to pick up Jack Phillips' distress call. Both the *Mount Temple* and the *La Provence* responded to the CQD message. But both were too far away to reach the stricken liner before she sank.

Captain Moore on the *Mount Temple* did alter course to head for the *Titanic* but encountered ice and had to slow down. By the time his ship reached the disaster, area the *Titanic* had sunk and any survivors still in the water were long since dead.

The distress call was also picked up at Cape Race, a radio listening station at Newfoundland. Cape Race, in turn, began to transmit the information that the *Titanic* was sinking. An American amateur radio enthusiast also picked up the distress call.

David Sarnoff operated a radio transmitter from the Wanamaker shop in New York. Now he too began to transmit details of the terrible life and death drama that was being enacted out on the dark, calm waters of the Atlantic. Around the world, numerous ships and other radio receivers now picked up the news that the *Titanic* was sinking. But all were powerless to intervene or help.

By now on the *Titanic* the squash court was flooded. More than 100 tons of water had entered the front parts of the ship. The bow rail was less than 5 metres above the surface of the freezing water.

On the deck the crew was beginning to muster around the lifeboats. Though the most senior officers on the ship were in charge, there was still great confusion. No proper lifeboat drills had been carried out.

Members of the crew were not allotted to any particular lifeboat. Now they rushed about taking up positions where they thought they were needed.

The lifeboats were eventually uncovered and lowered to the boat deck, ready for passengers to embark. When the passengers were safely in the boats, they would be lowered some 20 metres to the water.

By now the crew were notifying passengers of the emergency. They knocked on cabin doors and informed the occupants of the danger. Many passengers heeded the warning and made their way onto the open decks. Others simply refused to believe what they were being told and stayed in their beds.

Many passengers, aware of the impact and that the ship had stopped, came up on deck to see what had happened. Seeing the activity, they quickly realised that something was wrong but as yet had no idea of its seriousness. On the captain's orders, the crew were reassuring the passengers that there was no immediate danger. Thomas Andrews also went about reassuring passengers that all was well. He too was anxious to prevent panic.

Captain Smith was only too well aware of the possible consequences of panic breaking out, despite the crew's reassurances. He knew that evacuating the passengers would be difficult enough in the circumstances. But if there was a general panic, then it might become impossible and a great many lives might be lost as a result.

What was required was the creation of an air of calm. To achieve this, the captain had a brilliant idea. He would have the ship's orchestra come up to the First Class lounge on the promenade deck and play music there.

The members of the orchestra were summoned. Carrying their instruments and led by their leader, Wallace Hartley, the eight musicians made their way up onto A deck. Here, in the First Class lounge, they began to play ragtime music, which was extremely popular at the time. Their repertoire would have included the famous tune, 'Alexander's Ragtime Band'.

It was without doubt their most unusual performance and one that would go down in history. Little did they know, as they began to play, that it would be the last time they would ever play together and that all eight were destined to drown that very night. They displayed great bravery during the disaster and emerged as heroes of the *Titanic* tragedy.

The scene on the ship was now unreal. On the boat deck, the lifeboats were being readied. The radio was continually transmitting the distress call. More and more passengers were coming up on deck, many of them unsuitably dressed for such a cold night. Certainly those still in their nightclothes, along with many others, were not prepared to abandon the comfort and apparent safety of the ship and take to the small, wooden lifeboats.

Even yet, despite all the activity pointing to an emergency, most passengers still could not accept that the ship would sink. Though the bow had already sunk quite low in the water, this was still hardly noticeable on board.

Some passengers did prepare to evacuate the ship and returned to their cabins to dress properly. Others gathered at the purser's office to retrieve valuables left in the safe there. But as yet there was no air of general panic. The happy music drifting on the night air seemed to be having the desired effect.

Captain Smith was still hopeful that a ship could come to their aid. A German liner, the *Frankfurt* did respond to the distress call. But it was 170 miles away. Then they got a response from the liner, the *Carpathia*. It would come to their aid. Bride, the second wireless operator, brought this message to the bridge to Captain Smith.

For a moment there seemed to be hope. Smith went to the radio room and asked Phillips to find out how far away the ship was. When the position of the ship was radioed back, all hope faded. The *Carpathia* was 58 miles away. By the time it reached them the *Titanic* would be at the bottom of the ocean.

Captain Smith returned to the bridge. Now he was faced with giving an order that no ship's captain would ever wish to give. Taking a deep breath, he turned to his chief officer, Wilde, and spoke the words that banished all hope for the *Titanic*, its passengers and crew. They were the words that all those who travelled on board any vessel dreaded – the two words: 'Abandon ship!'

11

A GLIMMER OF HOPE

The *Carpathia* was now the only hope of rescue for the *Titanic*'s survivors. But even that ship was too far away to reach the stricken liner before it sank. Arthur Rostron, the captain of the Cunard liner, the great rival shipping line to The White Star Line, was determined to do everything in his power to help though.

On the sea, there is no rivalry when disaster strikes. Sailors know that they rely on their fellow sailors in times of danger. Every sailor on every ship is willing to risk his life for his fellow seamen.

It was by a stroke of good luck (one of the very few

to come the *Titanic's* way that night) that the *Carpathia* was able to come to the rescue. Unlike the *Titanic*, there was only one radio operator on the *Carpathia*. He was Harold Cottam and he was just 21 years old.

He had been on duty all that Sunday and around midnight was preparing to go off duty and retire to bed. He was aware that there were a number of messages for the *Titanic* coming through from Cape Race and on impulse he decided to try and contact the ship. But before he could complete his own message, asking if the ship was aware of the messages, which were coming through from Cape Race, the *Titanic* broke in with a startling message of its own.

This message was both stark and shocking. 'MGY. Come at once. We have struck an iceberg. Are sinking. CQD. Position 41.46N, 50.14S.'

At first Cottam could hardly believe what he had just heard. He asked for confirmation and quickly realised that he had heard correctly. The *Titanic* was sinking. There was no time to lose. Minutes, even seconds now, might count.

Cottam immediately rushed to the bridge with the message. Here, the officer of the watch took the radio operator to see the captain, who had retired for the night to his cabin.

Captain Arthur Rostron acted immediately. His subsequent behaviour and that of his crew that night was exemplary. After quickly making his way to the bridge, he worked out that his ship was about 58 miles from the disaster area.

He ordered that the *Carpathia* alter course towards the *Titanic*. Aware that time was of the essence, he demanded that his ship achieve maximum speed. Down in the boiler rooms and engine room the stokers, firemen and engineers began to work frantically.

Coal was shovelled into the boilers. Steam pressure rose until the gauges were on the edge of the red danger area. The up and down movement of the engines' gigantic pistons increased. The propellers began to spin more quickly, driving the great ship through the water. Slowly the *Carpathia* reached a speed close to 18 knots, far beyond what it was originally designed for.

While the ship raced across the ocean, other preparations for an emergency were also made. The crew was placed on immediate alert. The ship's lifeboats were readied in case they were needed. Hot food was also prepared, as were blankets and dry clothing.

Emergency lighting was rigged up. The ship's doctors got ready to deal with passengers who would have been exposed to the bitter cold. Captain Rostron posted extra lookouts. Harold Cottam, though suffering from fatigue after a long day, returned to his radio room.

For the next two hours he listened to the *Titanic's* distress calls. They were becoming more and more desperate by the minute. All information was conveyed to Captain Rostron on the bridge. As each message was relayed, the captain was becoming more aware that time was running out and that right now he was the *Titanic's* only hope. He was doing all he could but in the circumstances he knew that it would not be enough.

Back on the *Titanic*, Captain Smith issued the order to begin loading the passengers into the lifeboats. Aware that the lifeboats could not accommodate all the passengers and crew, he ordered that women and children should be loaded first.

Second Officer Lightoller took charge of the evacuation of the passengers on the port side. First Officer Murdoch took charge on the starboard side. Even now there was confusion among the officers. Despite the captain's orders, Murdoch, for reasons that will now never be known, forbade his colleague to begin the evacuation.

Lightoller, aware that time was running out, requested permission from the captain to begin the operation. This was promptly granted and Lightoller began his task. Lifeboat Number 4 was lowered from the boat deck to A deck from where it would be easier to load the passengers.

But some months previously, at the orders of Bruce Ismay, this deck had been enclosed by windows. This was to prevent spray from soaking passengers who might wish to sit there and look out on the ocean. Now, the windows could not be opened and the tool to open them could not be found.

This was not a very promising start and only mirrored the confusion that would occur throughout the unfolding tragedy. Without previous training or planning for such an emergency, it was inevitable that confusion would occur.

Lightoller decided to leave lifeboat Number 4 where it was for now and moved on to lifeboat Number 6. With the crew still confused and not all yet mustered, passengers began to assist in the loading.

One passenger who helped was Colonel Gracie. A soldier, trained to act in difficult conditions, he was just the sort of man needed in an emergency. Despite the perilous situation, he had managed to retain his sense of humour.

Shortly after the collision, on meeting the squash coach, Frederick Wright, Colonel Gracie suggested that they cancel their planned game arranged for the next day. By this time the squash court was actually flooded and Gracie must have known even then that the ship was doomed.

Some crew members did show initiative. Charles

Joughin, the ship's baker, gathered bread and handed it out to the crew to be divided among the lifeboats. Then he helped with the loading of the passengers.

When any passenger refused to enter the boats, Joughin used his initiative again and pushed them on board. Ordered to take charge of Lifeboat Number 10, thus being offered the chance to save his own life, he decided that he would be better occupied by remaining on board. Also, he felt that by leaving on the lifeboat he would be showing a bad example.

Other crew members, along with Thomas Andrews, still went about trying to reassure the passengers. This was now becoming necessary. The air of calm, which had prevailed at the beginning, was now being shattered. Evidence of this was most obvious on the lower decks where the Third Class passengers' accommodation was situated.

Here now there could be no doubt that the ship was mortally damaged. The water level was rising quickly, even advancing up the stairwells. Passengers were quickly emerging from their cabins taking with them what possessions they could carry.

Belonging to so many nationalities, most of them did not speak English. The crew was having problems trying to explain that only women and children were being allowed on deck right now. This was causing great distress, as families did not wish to be separated.

These passengers, many of whom came from small villages and rural areas, were also confused by the size of the ship. Most did not know how to reach the upper decks. Many of the access points leading into Second and First Class areas were blocked off by locked steel gates or locked doors.

As people found themselves trapped, they began to panic. At times the situation descended into farce. One passenger, after breaking down a locked door, was informed by a steward that he would have to pay for the damage. Others were too frightened to damage the ship by forcing open locked doors and rushed about the lower passageways panicked, confused and frightened.

On the famous passageway, which ran the length of the ship and was named Scotland Road by the crew, passengers also milled about. While some struggled towards the stern, others headed for the bow, all of them desperate to get to the outer decks but unsure of how to reach there.

Second and First Class passengers on the upper decks had easier access to the boat deck. Many, after collecting their valuables, made their way there. Those who might have been uncertain of the serious-ness of the situation soon realised that there was a very real emergency. Not only were the lifeboats being lowered but it was becoming obvious that the ship was going down at the bow. The decks were now visibly tilting, as were the stairways.

Even yet, many of the passengers were unsuitably dressed. Some were still in their nightclothes. Others had dressed inadequately in light clothing. Now many returned to their cabins and put on warmer clothes.

As more and more passengers arrived on the outside decks, Captain Smith became worried that matters might get out of hand. He decided to arm his officers. But here again confusion reigned. No one knew where the guns were kept. Eventually the guns were located and the officers were armed.

At this point Captain Smith went to the radio room. He was hoping that they could raise the *Olympic*, which was actually sailing from New York to Europe. If it was close and could come to their aid, then many lives might be saved.

It was while Smith was in the radio room that Harold Bride suggested that Phillips begin transmitting the distress call, SOS, instead of CQD. SOS (the letters did not stand for save our souls as was often thought) had been adapted some years before as a new distress call because of the greater ease with which the three letters could be tapped out in Morse code.

Phillips accepted Bride's suggestion and for the first

time ever, the distress call, SOS, was transmitted from a stricken ship. But would it bring hope to the *Titanic* and her passengers before it was too late? According to Thomas Andrews, the *Titanic* would only survive for two hours at most. Already three-quarters of an hour had passed since then. Time was running out.

12

THE MYSTERIOUS SHIP

Down in boiler room Number 5, order had been restored. The men working there were even beginning to have hope again. The watertight bulkhead was holding. The pumps were coping with the water that was now flooding in from boiler room Number 6.

Then disaster struck. Without warning, the bulkhead between Number 6 and Number 5 boiler room collapsed, possibly weakened by the earlier fire. Whatever the reason, tons of water now burst into the boiler room.

Most of the men working there escaped through the emergency hatches. But one of the engineers, Jonathan

Shepherd, had broken his leg when he had fallen down an open manhole. Now his colleague Herbert Harvey tried to save him. But his heroic efforts were in vain and both men drowned. They were the first officers to die in the disaster but Herbert Harvey would not be the only person to show great bravery that night.

With boiler room Number 5 now flooded, the situation was becoming even more urgent. The pumps could no longer cope. It would only be a matter of time before boiler room Number 4 began to flood.

On deck the evacuation of the passengers was now underway. But there was still great confusion and much incompetence. Lifeboat Number 7 was the very first to be launched. Here, Murdoch was in charge on the starboard side. He lowered the boat with only 27 people on board. The boat could hold 65.

Why there were only 27 passengers on the boat is a mystery. Was it because Murdoch was worried that the davits would not be able to take the weight of a fully-loaded boat? Did he think that once it was in the water, it could take on other passengers? Or was it because at that point passengers were still reluctant to leave the large unsinkable ship for a small and seemingly flimsy wooden lifeboat?

All these factors could explain Murdoch's actions. Witnesses later stated that passengers were reluctant to board the lifeboats. Women did not wish to be separated from their husbands. Perhaps this was the reason Murdoch allowed men to board the boats that night, despite the captain's orders that women and children were to be evacuated first.

The lifeboat was lowered some 20 metres to the smooth sea below. As it descended, passengers could see the interior of the ship through the portholes. Lights still blazed brightly in the luxurious cabins and fabulous lounges. Everything seemed perfectly normal, with the cheerful music from the orchestra drifting on the cold night air. Only the ship's bow lying low in the water gave a lie to this air of normality.

Suddenly the lights of another ship were sighted. Hope was rekindled. Officer Boxhall, who was on the bridge, sighted the lights of the vessel off the *Titanic*'s bow. He estimated that it was about 5 miles away.

Immediately he informed Captain Smith. It was virtually the first piece of good news that the captain had heard that night. There was still hope. A ship was close by and could come to the rescue. Smith ordered Boxhall to try contacting the ship by Aldis lamp. 'Signal that we are sinking,' he said, 'and that they must come quickly to our aid.'

The crew were not the only ones to see the ship's lights. Colonel Gracie also saw them. He even pointed them out to other passengers. Help was at hand. A ship was coming to rescue them. The news spread among those on deck. They were all going to be saved.

Boxhall immediately began signalling the ship. But it did not respond. Again and again Boxhall attempted to contact the ship but without success. For a moment he thought he had seen a response but realised it was probably the twinkling of a mast light.

Just then, an astonished quartermaster, George Rowe, contacted Boxhall. Rowe was on watch at the stern of the boat and reported that he had seen a lifeboat on the starboard side of the ship. Such was the confusion on board that Rowe had been completely forgotten about and was unaware of what was happening on deck.

Boxhall explained the situation and ordered Rowe to come to the bridge and bring emergency rockets with him. Boxhall intended trying to attract the attention of the nearby ship by firing the rockets high into the night sky.

Rowe arrived on the bridge and set up the rocket launcher on the bridge railing of the boat deck. Captain Smith ordered that a rocket be fired at five-minute intervals. Rowe fired the first rocket. It soared 800 feet into the dark sky. Here it burst into a brilliant white light, which punctured a hole in the darkness. But the ship still did not respond. Minutes later, it disappeared from sight.

Even today mystery still surrounds the presence of this ship. Did it actually exist? Were those who claimed to see its lights mistaken? This seems unlikely. Many saw the lights, including very experienced seamen like Captain Smith and Officer Boxhall.

So if the ship existed why did it not respond to the signals and the rockets? Was it engaged in some form of illegal activity? The chief officer of a Norwegian ship, the *Samson*, swore shortly before his death that it was his ship that was seen that night. They had been engaged in illegal fishing for seals in the area.

Thinking that the rockets were warnings from a coastguard ship to heave to and be inspected, they fled. Official records, however, show that this ship was fishing near Iceland at the time. So unless the records were falsified, the *Samson* could not be the mystery vessel. Today, the identity of the ship still remains a puzzle, one that will probably never be solved.

Seeing the rockets, any passengers with doubts about the danger they were in now began to realise the seriousness of the situation. Many knew that the *Titanic* had been in radio contact with other ships in the area, some of which were now coming to their aid. But if those ships were going to reach the stricken liner in time to save those on board, why was there a need to fire distress rockets?

It began to dawn on the passengers that it was likely that no ship would arrive in time. The captain, in desperation, was now trying to attract the attention of any ship in the area which might reach them and avert a disaster.

What they couldn't know was that the ship best placed to carry out a rescue effort – the *Californian* – did see the distress rockets. Chief Officer Stone was on the bridge and saw the rockets light up the night sky. He thought that they might be fireworks. At that time liners did put on firework displays for the passengers.

Despite this conclusion, Stone reported what he had observed to Captain Lord. Lord ordered Stone to try and contact the ship by signal lamp. Stone did so but the other ship did not respond.

At the inquiry held into the sinking of the *Titanic*, Captain Lord disputed this version of events. He contradicted what his officers said, including the testimony of Stone and another seaman called Gibson. But despite this, much of the blame for the disaster was placed on Lord's shoulders. He was made a scapegoat for the disaster and was later sacked by the Leyland Shipping Company which owned the *Californian*.

So while the *Californian* took no action, the situation on the *Titanic* was becoming more desperate. By now the card players were aware that the ship was going to sink. They abandoned their card game and left the lounge to get their life-jackets.

Down in the crew's quarters, the water was steadily rising. It was flooding Scotland Road, which now was all but deserted. The lights still burned but with the engines no longer operating, an eerie silence seemed to pervade the ship.

Water was beginning to enter boiler room Number 4. The pumps were operating but were hardly able to cope. Eventually the boiler room would flood and have to be abandoned.

Throughout the ship, the reality of what was happening was becoming more obvious by the minute. The bow was sinking lower and lower in the water. Time was running out for all of those still on board.

13

TO THE LIFEBOATS

On the boat deck, the evacuation of the passengers continued. Lifeboat Number 5 was launched from the starboard side with 40 people aboard. During the launch, Bruce Ismay strode about waving his arms and blurting out orders.

Instead of helping, he was hindering the operation and getting in the way. Officer Lowe, who was assisting with the launch, ordered Ismay to stop interfering. Surprisingly, the actual owner of the ship obeyed Lowe's order and ceased to interfere.

Margaret Brown, later to become known as 'The Unsinkable Molly Brown', was one of about twenty women passengers on this boat. The other twenty passengers were men. On the starboard side, from which this boat was launched, the order of women and children first was not strictly obeyed.

The quartermaster, Robert Hitchens, and the lookout, Frederick Fleet, were put in charge of this boat. Captain Smith ordered them to row towards the lights of the ship, which could still be seen in the distance. Once the passengers had been taken on board this vessel, the lifeboat was to return to pick up more survivors.

Was the ship Smith referred to the mystery ship Boxhall had seen? Or was there yet another ship in the area? Or was Smith mistaken, like so many others who had seen the lights? Yet again, there is no answer to this mystery.

As the boat was being lowered, a volunteer from among the passengers with sailing experience was asked to come forward to help man the boat. Major Peuchen, a yachtsman, volunteered. By now, the boat was already being lowered. But so anxious was Peuchen to avail of this opportunity to escape that he climbed down a rope to get onto the boat.

As the boats were being loaded, heartbreaking scenes were witnessed on deck. Families were separated. Husbands persuaded their wives and children to get onto the boats, then stepped back into the crowds on the deck. Many of those were certainly aware that they would never see their loved ones again but were determined to act with honour.

In the confusion, women were separated not only from their husbands but also from their children. Many women were bundled into boats without their children. Children too found themselves in boats without any parent or relative. As the boats were then lowered, adults and children were heard crying and screaming for their loved ones. Above the cries and wails of despair, the music from the ship's orchestra wafted out on the night air. But it could no longer quell the rising panic.

As lifeboat Number 8 was being loaded, a small drama took place – it was just one of many that took place that night. This involved an elderly married couple, Isidor and Ida Straus. When it was Ida's turn to take her place in the lifeboat, she refused to be separated from her husband.

The Straus couple were wealthy First Class passengers. Isidor was part owner of Macy's, the most famous of all New York's department stores. They had been together since their wedding day and now they had decided they would die together rather than be separated.

Crew members and other passengers tried to persuade Ida to get into the boat. But she still refused to do so. Colonel Gracie now tried to persuade Isidor to go with his wife. He was an old man and no one would think ill of him if he took a place in the boat.

But Isidor was determined that women and children should be saved first. He was in complete agreement with Captain Smith's order. Isidor and his wife were old. Their lives were almost at an end. It would be best if some younger persons had the opportunity to be saved, some who still had their whole lives ahead of them.

Ida Straus made sure that her maid, Ellen Bird, did get into the lifeboat. Ida also gave Ellen her fur coat to keep her warm. Then Ida joined her husband and they sat on two deck chairs and held hands. Both were drowned that night when the ship went down.

As lifeboat Number 8 was being lowered, there was another small drama. A young woman jumped out, shouting that she must get a photograph from her cabin. Two sailors caught her and bundled her back into the boat, almost certainly saving her life.

Also on lifeboat Number 8 was Lady Lucy-Noel Martha, the Countess of Rothes. She was a formidable woman and not only helped to row the boat but also helped to comfort those on board who were suffering from shock and the bitter cold.

In contrast to the Straus' selfless act of bravery and the courage of the Countess of Rothes, the action of Sir Cosmo and Lady Duff-Gordon seems cowardly indeed. They were a wealthy couple travelling First Class and were well-known celebrities in London. Both got into lifeboat Number 1 along with their secretary.

Sir Cosmo gave each crewman in the lifeboat £5, a large sum of money in 1912. Some claimed this was a bribe to save his life and that of his wife. However, Sir Cosmo claimed that it was to compensate the sailors for the loss of their kit and their belongings.

At the inquiry, it was alleged that the money was a bribe to the sailors on the lifeboat to persuade them not to return to the *Titanic* to pick up further survivors. It seemed that Sir Cosmo was worried that if they returned to pick up survivors, too many would attempt to get onto the boat. If that happened, the boat would sink and all on board would be drowned.

This fear was perfectly justified. Yet it was heartless and cowardly to refuse to return and help others. The Duff-Gordon's were disgraced by their behaviour and were afterwards shunned by many who had formerly admired them.

Not many on board the *Titanic* that night, whether wealthy or not, behaved like the Duff-Gordons and resorted to bribery. Many, in fact, were selfless just like the elderly Straus couple. One couple that did show great courage was Colonel John Jacob Astor and his wife Madeleine.

Colonel Astor was one of the richest men in America

and both he and his wife were travelling First Class. While the boats were being loaded, the couple went to the gymnasium and sat on the exercise machines. Here they calmly waited for their turn to escape the sinking ship. At no time did Colonel Astor try to use his wealth or influence to obtain a place on a lifeboat, either for himself or his wife.

At this time it was mostly First Class passengers, along with some of those from Second Class, who were being put on the boats. So far, not a single Third Class passenger had yet got onto a lifeboat.

For the most part, the crew ignored the safety of Third Class passengers. Some crew members did carry out their duty and led some Third Class passengers onto the boat deck. Yet other crew members prevented Third Class passengers from making their way to the upper decks.

Many of those who made their way to the upper decks were Irish. Most of them were Catholics. They gathered with other fellow passengers in the Third Class lounges to pray and say the rosary.

But at this stage, a great many Third Class passengers were still down on the lower decks. They were unable to, or were prevented from, finding a means of reaching the upper decks where there was some hope of salvation. Trapped in the depths of the ship, many would soon die as the water level continued to rise, metre by metre.

14

PANIC ON BOARD

The orchestra had by now moved out of the lounge onto the open deck. The musicians had put on their overcoats and life-jackets. The music gave an eerie and unreal feeling to the life and death battle, taking place around the musicians.

Despite the cheerful music, which up to now had helped calm the passengers, panic was beginning to set in. The ship was sinking at the bow minute by minute as thousands of litres of water continued to pour in through the gash in its hull.

As passengers were loaded onto the lifeboats,

poignant scenes continued to be seen. Reverend Robert James Bateman, on being separated from his sister-in-law, removed his tie and threw it down to her as a memento.

Another passenger, a gambler travelling under an assumed name, passed a hastily written note to a woman in one of the lifeboats. It read: 'If saved, inform my sister, Mrs F.J. Adams of Findlay, Ohio. Love, J.L. Rogers.'

All around, terrible scenes of distress were being enacted. Families were still being separated as women and children were put into the boats. Their cries of despair mingled with the music and the sound of exploding rockets.

On the *Californian*, the exploding rockets were still visible and another report was made to Captain Lord. But again he took no action. Why he did not get his radio operator, Evans, to try and contact the ship seems incomprehensible.

But at this time, passengers mostly used radio to contact the outside world. Therefore, on many ships, the radio was not manned on a 24-hour basis. Evans, the radio operator on the *Californian*, had been on duty all day that Sunday. Perhaps Captain Lord did not wish to disturb the man's sleep.

Whatever the reason, the *Californian* remained where she was. Unknown to Captain Lord and his crew, just a few miles away, people were now dying. Many were already dead. Many, many more would die before the dawn.

On the *Titanic* the situation was becoming more and more desperate. The bow was so low in the water that the name *Titanic* was now level with the waterline. Captain Smith, aware of the perilous situation and also aware that most of the lifeboats were only half full, tried to recall them to pick up more passengers. But not a single boat returned.

Thomas Andrews was also aware of the desperate situation. He moved among the passengers, urging women and children into the lifeboats. He also spoke to the crew in the hope of maintaining calm.

But there was still great confusion and many passengers had narrow escapes even before they entered the lifeboats. One woman slipped as she was getting into a boat. She would have plunged head first to her death if a fast-acting sailor had not grabbed her ankles. He held her until others came to his aid and they were able to pull her up and help her into the boat.

Some men, both crew and passengers, jumped into the lifeboats as they were being lowered. One man broke a woman's ribs by jumping into a lifeboat. Many others received cuts and bruises. But it was a small price to pay in return for your life.

Lifeboat Number 10 was launched from the port side with 47 people on board. Then lifeboat Number 5 was launched from the starboard side with 54 on board. By now, Murdoch and Lightoller and the other officers were no longer worried that the davits and cables would take the weight. It was becoming imperative to get as many off the ship as quickly as possible.

Officer Lowe was in charge of lowering lifeboat Number 5. As it was being lowered, he had to fire his pistol in the air to prevent passengers on G deck from jumping into the boat. By now all those on the ship knew that she was doomed. They were also becoming aware that the lifeboats could not take everyone. As these two facts became obvious, people became more and more desperate to save their lives.

Despite the fact that the ship was sinking and that water was flooding the lower decks, the electricity still functioned. This was due to the heroic work of Chief Engineer Bell and his men.

They had rigged up pipes and pumps to clear the water from boiler room Number 4 so that they could keep the electrical generators running. For a while the pumps coped with the water pouring in. But when it rose to the men's waists, they had to abandon the boiler room and move to the next one. Soon, water began to enter boiler room Number 3. Time and hope were slowly but surely running out.

In the radio room, Phillips continued to tap out the distress call, SOS. By now many ships were responding to the call. But all were too far away to be of any help. And there was still much confusion.

The radio operator on the *Olympic* did not appear to fully understand the situation and asked for more information. Perhaps this was understandable due to the fact that the *Titanic* was generally regarded as unsinkable.

Phillips became angry at this point. He knew that the *Titanic* would soon sink and that the only hope for the passengers and crew was that he might contact a ship that could come to their assistance.

Phillips had not put on a life-jacket. Now Harold Bride fitted him with one. But in the intense situation, Phillips was hardly aware of Bride's presence. Instead he kept sending the distress call, still hoping for a miracle.

By now it was becoming obvious that a miracle was required. The *Titanic* was listing. The angle of the decks was becoming steeper as the bow sank even deeper into the water. It was becoming more difficult to stand upright.

Lifeboats Number 12, with 32 on board, and Number 9, with 48 on board, were launched. Men, mostly from the crew, were then found hiding under a tarpaulin in lifeboat Number 14. Officer Lowe, now on the lifeboat, again drew his pistol and ordered them off. With the assistance of some passengers, they were forcibly removed.

As the boat was being loaded, Edward Ryan, a passenger, disguised himself as a woman. With a shawl wrapped about his head and shoulders, he took a place in the boat and was saved. Nearby a group of men were ready to rush the boat and get on board.

Seaman Joseph Scarrott, aware of this, grabbed a boat's tiller and waved it threateningly to keep the men back. Lowe again fired his pistol in the air to try to maintain order.

As Number 14 was being lowered, the cables jammed. The boat hung perilously out over the sea. Again Joseph Scarrott came to the rescue. With his knife, he cut the jammed cables and the boat dropped a metre or so to the water. Despite the jar of the impact, no one on board was injured.

As lifeboat Number 11 was being loaded, Steward James Witter was saved by a quirk of fate. As he was helping a female passenger into the boat, both stumbled and fell in. Witter was about to get out when Murdoch ordered him to stay where he was. He would be needed to help row when the boat was lowered.

Still the lights blazed brightly. Still the music wafted on the cold night air. But now the liner was listing badly. Water was lapping at the foot of the crow's nest where just two hours before Fleet had rung the bell to warn of the iceberg.

Thomas Andrews' prediction was coming true. Right now the *Titanic* had little more than half an hour remaining before she slipped beneath the mirror-smooth surface of the Atlantic.

15

COURAGE AND COWARDICE

anic had now taken over. People were sobbing and crying. From the lower decks came the helpless screams and pleas of Third Class passengers who were still trapped.

The decks were now dangerously tilted, as were the stairways. At the stern, the tips of the blades of the giant propellers were just becoming visible above the waterline.

Lifeboat Number 13 was now launched with 54 on board. Half of those were Third Class passengers, the largest group from that class to be rescued. Among them was the young Irishman, Daniel Buckley.

One lucky family also got on this boat. They were

Sylvia Caldwell, her husband Albert and their ten-month old son Alden. Despite being Second Class passengers, they got lost below and could not reach the upper decks.

A group of passengers on the boat deck spotted them and lowered a ladder. The family were then able to climb up to the boat deck. Sylvia and Alden got on lifeboat Number 13 and Albert jumped in to join them as the boat was being lowered.

Paul Mauge, the *Titanic*'s restaurant manager, also jumped into this boat. He was just one of many of the ship's crew who saved themselves. But overall, most of the crew behaved in a courageous manner.

While lifeboat Number 13 was being lowered, it almost met with a disaster. Close to the surface, a jet of water was gushing from a scupper. This caught the boat and pushed it back towards the stern of the ship.

Just at that moment, lifeboat Number 15 was being lowered at the stern. Those in Number 13 now found themselves directly beneath the other boat. It would come down on top of them and crush everyone on board.

The passengers on Number 13 immediately began to scream a warning. But in the noise and confusion, they could not be heard. Slowly the boat came lower and lower. Now those standing up in Number 13 could touch the bottom of Number 15 with their fingertips.

All on board lifeboat Number 13 seemed doomed. But the quick action of two sailors on the boat saved all their lives. Leaping to their feet, they dashed to either end of the boat and cut the cables. The jet of water now swept the boat away just in time.

No sooner had it moved away than Number 15 landed in the sea on the very spot where Number 13 had been. For once the number thirteen did not prove unlucky even if those on the boat had a narrow escape. For the Caldwell family especially, their luck was still holding up.

Some stokers got away on this boat. Used to working in the intense heat of the boiler rooms, they usually only wore shorts and vests. Now they found themselves inadequately dressed for such a bitterly cold night.

Also on this boat was twelve-year-old Ruth Becker. While on deck waiting to get onto a lifeboat, her mother had sent her back to their cabin to get some blankets. They would need them later when they were on an open lifeboat on the sea.

While Ruth was away, her mother, sister and brother were bundled into lifeboat Number 11. So when Ruth returned with the blankets, she found herself alone on deck. She did not know where her family was or what had happened to them.

Luckily a sailor bundled her into lifeboat Number 13

still clutching her two blankets. Now, despite her ordeal, and not knowing the fate of her family, she willingly gave up the blankets. These were then cut up and given to the shivering stokers to wrap about themselves. This probably helped to save their lives.

This was just one of the many acts of courage and generosity that were to prevail that night. And while many adults like Edward Ryan and Paul Mauge behaved in a disgraceful manner, a distraught twelve-year-old girl behaved with great honour and dignity.

Lifeboat Number 15, which almost caused the disaster to Number 13, had 57 people on board. Among them was Eugene Daly. He was the piper who had played 'Erin's Lament' as the *Titanic* sailed away from Cobh. He could not have imagined then that he would be lamenting the deaths of 1,503 people a few days later.

Now, the first of the collapsible boats was lowered. This was Boat C with 32 persons on board. Reports afterwards claimed that Murdoch, who was in charge of lowering this boat, fired his pistol at some men who intended rushing it and taking it over. The claims stated that one man was killed and that Murdoch then shot himself.

Others claimed that this was not true and that Murdoch behaved like a true officer should, with honour and courage. What is known is that Purser McElroy was forced to fire his pistol to restore order while the boats were being lowered. Perhaps it was this incident that people remembered. There is no record that McElroy killed anyone and certainly he did not shoot himself.

Collapsible Boat C contained one passenger whose courage and behaviour that night would be called into question in the aftermath of the sinking. This man was none other than Joseph Bruce Ismay, chairman of the White Star Line and the owner of the *Titanic*.

Even still much controversy surrounds his behaviour that night. Many continue to blame him for the disaster and claim that he had ordered Captain Smith to maintain speed despite the presence of icebergs in the area. What is known is that he kept a warning about the presence of icebergs to himself for many hours that Sunday.

He had also tried to interfere with officers during the loading of the lifeboats and was ordered away by Officer Lowe. But this may have stemmed from a genuine motive to assist as best he could. Now, however, he got on board Collapsible Boat C. Some claim that he acted in a cowardly manner and got into the boat to save himself. Others claim that he was bundled into the boat by Murdoch.

Whichever is the truth of the matter, he certainly took his place in the boat while others stood back, knowing that they would die. Thomas Andrews chose this fate for himself. He was last seen in the First Class lounge, staring at a painting entitled 'Arriving in the New World'. He had removed his life-jacket and when asked by a steward that he put the jacket back on, ignored the request. He did not speak and seems to have decided to go down with the ship he had designed.

Lifeboat Number 2 was lowered next with twenty on board, half the number it could carry. Officer Boxhall was in charge of this boat. He had the foresight to take with him some green signal rockets. These he later fired when the *Carpathia* arrived on the scene and so those on this boat were the first survivors to be picked up.

By now the end of the great liner was approaching. In the radio room Phillips still tapped out his distress call. Down in boiler room Number 2 the stokers and firemen were told to abandon their posts and try to save themselves.

The engineers and the electricians remained at their posts, determined to provide power to the electrical generators. It is a pointer to their dedication that not a single engineer survived the disaster. Without their commitment to keeping the electric generators working, many more would have died in the greater panic, which would surely have ensued if the ship had been in total darkness.

Lifeboat Number 4, the first to be lowered that night to A deck for ease of loading the passengers, was now hauled up onto the boat deck. In the confusion it was lowered once more to A deck and then hauled back up. During this manoeuvre, passengers were ordered down to A deck and then back up again to the boat deck. This naturally caused further confusion and panic.

One of those who took a place in this boat was Madeleine Astor. Colonel John Jacob Astor asked if he might join his wife in the boat and was refused permission to do so. Unlike Bruce Ismay, Astor stood back and did not use his wealth or influence to gain favour. He did not survive.

By now passengers and crew were well aware of the reality of the situation. The *Titanic* was doomed and there was no hope of getting off in the lifeboats. Their only hope lay in jumping into the water and swimming to one of the boats, which had already been launched.

Many did jump now, after first throwing deckchairs overboard so that they would have something to cling onto in the water. But others, like Colonel Astor and Thomas Andrews, calmly accepted their fate.

At this point the card players had returned to the lounge to quietly await theirs. Isidor and Ida Straus had returned to their cabin and there clung to each other. They were still determined to die together.

Benjamin Guggenheim, an American millionaire,

returned to his cabin with his manservant and dressed in his finest evening wear. He then returned on deck. Here he told a fellow passenger that he would never dream of using either his wealth or position to obtain a place in a boat. 'Never forget,' he said, 'that Benjamin Guggenheim died like a gentleman.'

By now the water level was only 3 metres below the Promenade deck. The bow railings were actually under water. Despite this, and the fact that the decks were now tilted at an acute angle, the orchestra still played on.

There has always been disagreement as to what exactly they were playing as the ship sank. Many witnesses claimed that it was the hymn, 'Nearer my God to Thee', an appropriate piece to play in the circumstances. Walter Hartley, the leader of the orchestra, is alleged to have once said that if he were ever in such a situation, it was this particular hymn he would play.

However, another passenger, Henry Wilson Barkworth, later claimed that the tune the orchestra played was the waltz, 'Autumn'. Colonel Gracie and Harold Bride confirmed this and certainly the waltz was part of the band's repertoire.

The mystery of what tune they actually did play as the ship sank will never now be resolved. What is not in doubt is that the eight men in the orchestra behaved with courage and honour. None survived and they died as so many others did that night, doing their duty right up to the end.

By now the *Titanic*'s end was in sight. Little hope remained for those still on the ship or those swimming in the water. For all of them, time was about to run out.

16

TITANIC SINKS

A t this point, the last lifeboat launched from the
Titanic was lowered to the water on the port side.
This was Collapsible Boat D. It had twenty people on
board, though it could carry 40.

Why there were only twenty on board was probably
due to the fact that it had to be launched in a hurry. By
now it was almost impossible to stand upright on the
tilted decks and it was becoming extremely difficult to
work in such conditions.

As this boat was being loaded, a Second Class passenger called Hoffman came forward with two children. He claimed that the children were his and they

were placed in the boat. Mr Hoffman then withdrew, accepting his own fate now that his children were safe.

Later, when the survivors arrived in New York, it was discovered that the man was not called Hoffman. He was, in fact, Michel Navratil and was travelling under the assumed name of Hoffman.

He had snatched the children from his wife. She had been living with her children in France and now their father was taking them back to New York to live with him. The children, Michel Marcel aged three and Edmond Roger aged two, did, in fact, survive. Their father, however, died in the tragedy.

Some passengers did jump into this boat as it was being lowered. Remaining passengers on the deck began to move towards the stern to avoid the water, which was rising much more quickly. By now, the fore-castle had disappeared under the waves.

Captain Smith visited the radio room and thanked Phillips and Bride for their endeavours that night and for their courage and dedication to duty. Now it was time for them to try and save their own lives. He also informed his crew that they had done their duty and that they could do no more. They too should now look to saving themselves.

Phillips, however, remained at his post and the last signal ever to be sent from the *Titanic* was picked up by the *Virginian*. At this point, the power began to fade. Lights flickered and went dim. But Phillips continued tapping out his SOS even though he must have been aware that there was insufficient power to transmit it.

At this point, Bride entered their sleeping quarters behind a curtain to collect some personal belongings. When he returned he found Phillips grappling with a crewman who was trying to rip the life-jacket from the radio operator.

With the assistance of Bride, the two men overpowered the assailant and left him unconscious in the radio room. Now, as the power faded, both men went out on deck. They could do no more.

On deck, desperate efforts were being made to free Collapsible Boat B from the roof of the officers' quarters. Why this boat and Boat A were not freed earlier and kept in readiness is another mystery. Again it seems to point towards the confusion that prevailed that night and to a lack of proper training and planning for the possibility that the ship might need to be evacuated in an emergency.

When the boat was eventually freed, it fell onto the deck upside down. As an attempt was made to right it, it was swept overboard by a huge wave which surged forward. Many people were also swept into the water.

Though the boat remained upside down, 30 people

swimming in the water managed to climb onto the keel over the next few minutes. They were lucky because all of them were later saved.

The final boat, Collapsible Boat A, was also freed. Its lashing proved difficult to undo and was cut by a knife supplied by Colonel Gracie. Right to the end Gracie was there, trying to assist as best he could.

But as the boat was freed, it was swamped by the huge surge of water. Twenty people managed to clamber into the waterlogged boat. Later, after the *Titanic* had sunk and Officer Lowe came to their assistance, eight of those on board had died from exposure.

By now passengers were jumping from the aft steerage door into the freezing water. This was a jump of more than 30 metres because by now the *Titanic*'s stern was rising up out of the water. Many were throwing in whatever objects they could find that might float and then jumping in after them.

One passenger manhandled a door over the side and then jumped in after it. Others, like Colonel Gracie, clung onto whatever was at hand, resigned now to whatever fate had in store for them.

At the aft end of the boat deck, Reverend Thomas Byles and a group of passengers gathered to pray. From within the ship came the sound of loud crashes and bangs as furniture began to move when the decks tilted towards the vertical. Crockery and glasses began to crash to the floors.

The propellers were now visible as the stern rose out of the sea. Captain Smith was sighted for the last time on the bridge. Then the funnel nearest the bow broke away and fell with a terrible crash. Those who were unfortunate enough to find themselves directly in its path were crushed to death.

The lights flickered and went out. The ship was plunged into darkness. Waves washed over the decks, sweeping Officers Wilde, Murdoch and Lightoller into the sea, along with Colonel Gracie.

Lightoller swam to the crow's nest, which was now almost totally under water, and managed to cling on. But realising that the ship would sink in minutes, he let go and tried to swim away.

He found himself trapped, however, against the iron grill of a ventilation shaft. The pressure of the water held him there as the bow sank further. He could not get away and was certain that he would die.

But as more water flooded into the ship, air was forced up the shaft. Lightoller was literally blown upwards to the surface and was able to swim away from the ship. Meanwhile, Colonel Gracie hung onto the roof of the officers' quarters. When he got his breath back, he too swam away from the ship.

By now it was impossible to stand upright on the decks. People clung on as best they could. But many, exhausted by the cold and their ordeal, lost their grip and began to slide down the decks into the water.

Then there came a most terrible grinding and tearing sound. The *Titanic*'s hull was splitting in two from the uppermost decks to the keel, between the third and fourth funnels. As the ship split in two, the bow slid beneath the waves. The stern rose until it was almost vertical, the propellers now pointing to the dark starry sky. Those passengers still on the decks now clung on desperately or fell into the water.

The stern flooded and began to sink. Colonel Gracie was sucked down with it. But he found an air bubble escaping from the sinking stern and managed to reach the surface. He swam to the upturned boat and clambered onto the keel.

One hundred metres down, the stern imploded due to the pressures and the air still trapped inside. Four massive explosions ripped through it. Then the surface of the sea was still again. Other than the cries of those in the boats and in the water, an eerie silence prevailed.

It was 2.20am on the morning of Monday 15 April 1912. Two hours and 40 minutes after the collision with the iceberg, the *Titanic* had disappeared beneath the Atlantic waves.

17

ADRIFT ON THE OCEAN

The *Titanic* was gone. The largest, finest and most luxurious ship ever to sail the seas was now at the bottom of the Atlantic Ocean. Many of those who had survived and were now in the lifeboats had watched the ship's demise. But some survivors, like Bruce Ismay, turned away as the *Titanic* sank. Ismay could not bear to watch as his dream ship disappeared beneath the water.

Those who watched did so with awe and fear. Those in the first lifeboats to be launched had watched the whole drama unfold. They had seen the ship with all its lights blazing lying still in the water. It seemed unscathed. Only the bow, now that little bit deeper in the water, gave any indication of the terminal wound the hull had received in the collision.

Over the next hour and a half they had watched the ship, still ablaze with light, slowly succumb to the power of nature. All the while, music drifted on the night air along with the shouts and cries of those on board. In those last moments, when the music stopped and the lights went out and the *Titanic* split in two and sank, they felt utterly helpless in the face of such a tragedy.

On the *Californian*, Stone and Gibson had also watched the tragedy and its end. They had even remarked to each other that ships did not usually fire rockets for no reason. They had also noted that the ship did not appear to sit correctly in the water.

But despite conveying their thoughts and worries to Captain Lord he did not take any action. Eventually the ship disappeared and both men thought it had sailed over the horizon. Again this information was conveyed to Lord but again he merely listened, turned over in his bunk and went to sleep.

But although the *Titanic* had now sunk, the tragedy was far from over. Those lucky enough to be in a lifeboat were already suffering from the bitter cold. Many were wet, and all were frightened and uncertain of their future.

But they were still the lucky ones. For those who were now in the water, wearing life-jackets or clinging onto bits of wreckage, the future was bleak. The water was below freezing point and no one could survive for long in that situation. Most of those in the water would be dead in 30 minutes or so from the cold. Even if they were rescued within 30 minutes, their chances of survival in an open boat, soaking wet and with no protection or warmth were poor.

They swam about or clung to wreckage, calling out for help. Their pitiless cries rang out starkly in the darkness. There were prayers too and entreaties to God to help them. But no help was forthcoming.

The two boats nearest to the disaster area were Collapsible Boats A and B. The stronger of the swimmers made their way to those two boats. Many climbed on board A until it drifted away and those in the water were no longer able to swim.

Officer Lightoller made it to upturned Collapsible Boat B and climbed onto the keel. Colonel Gracie had earlier swum to this boat and had also managed to clamber onto the keel. Harold Bride had become trapped beneath the boat and was desperately gasping for the little amount of air still trapped there.

Aware that he could not survive for much longer, he took one large breath, and kicked out with all his might.

He escaped what would have been his tomb, surfaced and clambered onto the keel.

Eventually 30 men clambered on, threatening to overturn or sink the boat with their weight. One swimmer drew close and asked if he could climb on. He was told that one more might sink the boat and drown everyone.

'That's all right, men,' he said. Then he swam off, but not before calling out: 'Good luck, God bless you.' Another swimmer who was close by kept calling out encouragement but made no attempt to get onto the keel nor did he ask for help. After a while he grew silent. Later, one of the men on the boat claimed that the man was none other than Captain Smith.

Whether it was or not no one can ever know. Someone else claimed that they saw Captain Smith rescue a child from the water. When he had placed the child in a boat, he then swam away. Again this story can never be confirmed.

The men on the upturned boat decided they should pray. Having many different religious beliefs, they eventually agreed that they would recite the Lord's Prayer. Their voices mingled with the cries of those still struggling for survival in the water.

While those on the upturned boat clung on for life and prayed, those already in the lifeboats were not much better off. Most were suffering from shock and exposure. Many of the crew from the stricken ship who were put on board to row and command the boat failed to carry out their duty. Either they too were in shock, or were not properly trained or prepared.

Or, perhaps, they were aware that from the moment the *Titanic* sank, they were no longer employees of the White Star Line. In fact their later wage slips would show that their employment ceased the moment the *Titanic* sank beneath the waves.

Almost all the lifeboats refused to return to the scene of the disaster to try and pick up survivors. Many people could have been saved if they had done so because most of the boats were only half full. But both crew and survivors were frightened to return. They feared that the hundreds of people who were in the water would swamp the boats and all would be lost.

On those boats, where the crew were ineffective, the passengers took charge. That night the Countess of Rothes behaved in an admirable fashion. She organised the women in the boat to row and she took the tiller herself. She also offered comfort to those who were in distress at the loss of their husbands or other loved ones.

Margaret Brown, 'The Unsinkable Molly Brown', also behaved admirably that night. This boat contained Quartermaster Hitchens and the yachtsman, Major

Peuchen. Rivalry developed between the two men when Hitchens insisted he was in charge. As a major used to giving orders, Peuchen thought he should be in charge.

Arguments broke out when Hitchens refused to return to pick up survivors. Instead the boat headed for the lights of the vessel which had been seen on *Titanic's* bow earlier that night. But when the lights disappeared, Hitchens declared that they were all lost. Peuchen too gave up.

Molly Brown now rallied the women on board to take over the oars. Hitchens pointed out that they had no compass and so could not plot a course. At this, Molly Brown pointed to the North Star. They would plot their course by the stars as sailors had done since man first took to the sea.

Hitchens, not happy at having his authority questioned, ordered the rowers to stop and allow the boat to drift. Molly Brown now threatened to throw him overboard if he did not shut up and cease his interference. Hitchens did shut up and the rowing continued with Molly Brown now in charge. The rowing not only occupied the women but also helped to keep them warm in the bitter cold.

In other boats too the physical exercise of rowing helped to keep the occupants warm. In one boat a women rowed all that night with her feet in freezing cold water.

Of all the lifeboats on the sea that night, only one

returned to try and pick up survivors. This was lifeboat Number 14 under the command of Officer Lowe. He had eventually rounded up some of the boats and tied them together. Then he shared out his survivors among these boats and headed back to the disaster area.

It was now nearly 3am and any survivors had been in the water for nearly 50 minutes. For Lowe and his crew, it was a terrible experience rowing among the dead and dying, and the debris of the wreck. They called out again and again in the dark but there was hardly any response.

In the end they picked up four people who were still alive, yet nearly all the lifeboats had room for many more.

By 3am the desperate cries of those in the water had ceased. A terrible silence hung over the sea. High above there was a tremendous display of shooting stars. The saying that each time a star falls a soul goes to heaven came to the mind of some of the survivors. They could not have known then that over 1,500 falling stars would be required on this tragic night.

There were 705 survivors, and 1,503 (the figure given at the inquiry into the disaster) died. It was the worst loss of life in a single ship disaster in the history of seafaring. Even in its demise, the *Titanic* was setting new records. But for those 705 who were still alive, their only thoughts were of continuing survival.

18
RESCUE!

While the passengers in the lifeboats struggled for survival in the bitter cold, the *Carpathia* headed for the disaster area at full steam. The last message from the *Titanic* had been received in the radio room at around 1.45am. It said: 'Come as quickly as possible, old man; engine room is filling up to the boilers.' The few stark words signified that the end of the ship was near.

Cottam stayed at his radio, listening for any further message. There were many from other ships that had heard the *Titanic*'s distress call. But the ship itself was now ominously silent.

Captain Rostron had already calculated that he

would not reach the disaster area before the *Titanic* sank. But he knew that every second counted for those who had survived. The sooner he reached them the better their chance of surviving.

Despite the warnings of ice, he maintained maximum speed. The vibration caused by the engines running at full revolutions alerted the passengers on board. At first they thought there was a problem with their own ship – perhaps there was a fire on board or they had struck an iceberg.

Those who got out of bed to check what was happening found the ship to be a hive of activity. This certainly was most unusual in the middle of the night. Passengers became fearful for their safety but were reassured there was no problem with the *Carpathia*. Instead they learned that the *Titanic* had struck an iceberg and was sinking.

Many of the passengers disbelieved the news. While they could accept that the *Titanic* might have struck an iceberg, they simply could not accept that she was in any danger. Why, the *Titanic* was unsinkable! Everyone knew that.

Still there could be in no doubt of the mood of urgency aboard the *Carpathia*. Something was seriously wrong. They were about to be involved in a massive drama. At that time none of them could have imagined the full horror that lay ahead.

On the bridge, Captain Rostron could do no more. His ship was now ready to deal with an emergency. He had an excellent crew and they were all on full alert. He had overlooked nothing in preparation for what lay ahead.

A little after 2.30am, Rostron saw the green light of a flare off the port bow. He thought that it must be from the *Titanic* and that despite his earlier fears she was still afloat. He felt a surge of hope that he might still reach the disaster area in time.

But shortly after that the first iceberg was spotted ahead. Then more and more icebergs appeared. Very soon the *Carpathia* was weaving its perilous way among them.

Rostron was well aware of the danger his own ship was facing right then. But he knew that if he slowed down then many of those on the *Titanic*, if she had not yet sank, would almost certainly die as a result. He ordered his men to keep an even sharper lookout, if that were possible, and to maintain full steam in the boilers.

The *Carpathia* now began firing rockets at fifteen-minute intervals. With the *Titanic*'s radio silent, this was the only way the liner could alert the stricken ship and those now in the lifeboats, that help was on the way. On board the *Carpathia*, the crew became tense. They were getting closer to the disaster area. Soon they would have to spring into action.

By 3.30am *Carpathia* was drawing close to the last known position of the *Titanic*. But still there was no visible sighting of her. Captain Rostron became more and more apprehensive. Could the unthinkable have happened and, despite the sighting of the green flares, she had already gone to the bottom of the ocean? It was a frightening thought.

At around 4am the *Carpathia* reached the disaster area. Rostron ordered that the engines be stopped and the ship slowly came to a standstill. There was no sign of the *Titanic* or indeed of any wreckage. Dawn would soon lighten the sky but as yet it was dark, with a rising wind and a swell on the sea.

Another green flare burst into the sky and in its light, Rostron saw a lifeboat in the water a short distance away. It now slowly manoeuvred up to the liner and made fast. In it were Fourth Officer Boxhall and 24 other survivors.

Apart from a brief exchange between Boxhall and Rostron, there was silence, except for the wailing of a baby. Rostron could easily make out the name printed on the lifeboat. It was *Titanic*. Even then, before it was officially confirmed, he knew that the ship had gone down.

A ladder was dropped down to the lifeboat. Then just after 4am, the first survivor of the disaster, Elizabeth

Allen, scrambled up to the safety of the ship. When asked what had happened to the *Titanic* she simply answered that she had sunk. The other survivors, still shocked and bitterly cold, now too scrambled to safety.

Keeping to the proper formalities even on such an occasion, Rostron met Boxhall on the bridge and officially asked him what had happened. '*Titanic* sank at 2.20am,' Boxhall explained, confirming what Rostron had already suspected.

By the time the lifeboat was empty, dawn was breaking. Now, in the half-light, those on board the *Carpathia* glimpsed the other lifeboats. They rode the choppy waves amongst hundreds of icebergs. Some of these icebergs were just small chunks of ice. But others towered 20 or 30 metres above the surface of the sea.

It was an awesome and chilling sight, like something out of a fairy tale set at the North Pole. But more chilling still, it was also an indication of how close the *Carpathia* itself had been to a disaster. Had she struck one of the bigger icebergs she could have been mortally damaged also.

Captain Rostron now noted that all the remaining lifeboats were in an area of about 4 square miles surrounding his own ship. His priority now was to get the survivors aboard the *Carpathia* as quickly as possible.

A sense of urgency pervaded. Many of the survivors

had been exposed to the bitter cold for between four and five hours. Many were soaked through and many more had inadequate clothing for the situation they found themselves in. All were suffering from shock and exhaustion.

Some survivors, like those on the keel of Collapsible Boat B, were in the most perilous of all positions. Right now they were still at least four miles from the safe haven of the *Carpathia*. Collapsible Boat B was still upturned and had slowly sunk lower in the water during the night. It had come close to actually sinking and leaving the desperate, stricken survivors floundering in the icy ocean.

Aware of this, Officer Lightoller, who had taken command, had ordered the men to stand upright. Then he had ordered them to sway with the movement of the boat on the swell. It was all they could do to try and stay afloat until help came.

Now their situation was absolutely desperate. They were cold, wet and exhausted. Even yet any hope of rescue from the *Carpathia* was still some time away. Aware that they could not stay afloat much longer, they began to shout for help. Then, mercifully, Lightoller found his whistle and blew it.

Two nearby boats heard the whistle and immediately responded. But even getting close to the upturned boat proved hazardous for those standing on it. It was so close to sinking that even the wash from the approaching boats could have sunk it.

However, the boats did get close enough to rescue the stricken men. Harold Bride and Colonel Gracie, along with the other men, were taken off. Lightoller, as befitting an officer, was the last man to leave his perilous perch. Now, safe at last, they began to row for the *Carpathia*.

Earlier that night, after searching for survivors, Officer Lowe had returned to his small flotilla of boats. But he found that they had scattered in the darkness. Two of them had gone to the rescue of the men standing on the keel of Collapsible Boat B. The others were heading for the *Carpathia*.

Lowe had hoisted a sail as the breeze freshened, the only person to do so that night. He noticed that Collapsible Boat D was low in the water. He went to her aid, got a line attached and began to tow her.

Next, he noticed Collapsible Boat A. It was almost swamped and was not moving. Again Lowe went to her rescue. She was on the verge of sinking and about a dozen persons, including one woman, were standing in water up to their knees.

Lowe took them all into his own boat and left the almost swamped boat. Now he set off for the *Carpathia*, still towing Collapsible Boat D. Ahead of him the other lifeboats were reaching the liner and the survivors were being taken aboard.

One by one, as the sun came up, the survivors clambered into the safety of the *Carpathia*. Here, they were given hot drinks and taken to change out of their soaked clothing. The passengers on the *Carpathia* readily gave some of their own clothing to the survivors.

The survivors were a bedraggled and for the most part, a silent group. They were dressed in a myriad of clothing styles with some still in their nightwear. Some women were wearing elaborate evening gowns. Others wore fur coats and capes while still others were wrapped in blankets. Some wore shoes, a few had bedroom slippers and there were some who were barefoot.

Many were unable to speak and the silence was intense, except for the odd cry or wail. Others just did not want to speak. Some were still too shocked to even be aware that they were now safe. And even if they could speak they had no words to convey what they had witnessed. It was simply too monstrous.

A great many had lost loved ones and friends that night. Women now found themselves without their husbands and were still not sure whether they were dead or alive. Families had been separated, many destined never to see again those they had lost. Worst of all were those who had lost children and there were many. But there were happy reunions too as families who were separated in the rescue were reunited. Among those who found their loved one was Ruth Becker.

Daniel Buckley and Eugene Daly were among those who reached the safe deck of the *Carpathia*. They would yet see New York and have the opportunity of a new life. Others were not to be so lucky.

Though he was saved, Bruce Ismay never recovered from the disaster. On reaching the *Carpathia*, he retired to a cabin and did not emerge until the liner reached New York. Though cleared at the inquiry of any blame, nevertheless, he was held to blame for the disaster by the media and the general public. The fact that he had taken a place in a lifeboat while other men chose to die rather than do so also went against him.

Less than a year after the sinking he retired from his position with The White Star Line and went to live in Ireland. He died in 1937, a broken man who in the intervening years had kept very much to himself. Like many of those who survived the disaster, he was to suffer the consequences for the rest of his life.

By 8am that morning, all the boats, except for one, had reached the *Carpathia* and the survivors had been taken on board. Now, Lifeboat Number 12 eventually reached the lee of the liner. Officer Lightoller, who had transferred to Lifeboat Number 12 from the upturned keel of Collapsible Boat B, was in command.

Lifeboat Number 12 now contained over 70 survivors and was almost swamped. Yet Lightoller, despite a few hair-raising moments, brought the boat into the shelter of the *Carpathia's* hull.

The survivors were brought on board. Colonel Gracie gave thanks for his rescue. Harold Bride collapsed on reaching the safety of the deck. Lightoller remained on the lifeboat until everyone was off. Then he too clambered up the ladder to safety. He was the most senior of all the *Titanic's* officers to survive and the last one to board the *Carpathia*.

With the arrival of Lightoller, 705 persons from the *Titanic* were now safe on the *Carpathia*. But there was hardly one among them, or among all those on the liner, who was not thinking of those others, 1,503 men, women and children, who had perished that very night in the dark waters of the Atlantic Ocean.

19

WORLD IS STUNNED

A board the *Californian*, the green rockets had been sighted during the night. But it was not until dawn that Captain Lord woke Evans. 'A ship has been firing rockets,' he said. 'Get on your radio and find out if anything is wrong.'

Evans was soon very much aware of what was wrong. With disbelief he listened to the messages coming in over the airwaves. Within moments the terrible news was conveyed to Captain Lord on the bridge. The news was stark. The *Titanic* had hit an iceberg and had sunk.

Lord immediately ordered that the engines should be started and a course struck for the last known position of the sunken ship. By the time he reached it, the *Carpathia* had already rescued all the survivors and was now searching the area where the *Titanic* had sunk one last time.

It was a fruitless search. No one could have survived for six hours in the bitter cold waters. But Captain Rostron felt it was his duty to search, just in case.

Now, with the *Californian* on the scene, that ship could continue the search and the *Carpathia* could set sail for New York. After a few sombre exchanges, the *Californian* began searching and the *Carpathia* turned its bows toward New York.

It took some time for the *Carpathia* to emerge from the ice field. During this time, Captain Rostron asked a clergyman, Reverend Father Anderson, to hold a religious service in the main lounge. Here, passengers and crew from both ships gathered to give thanks for those who had been saved and to pray for those who had died.

Once free of the ice field, the *Carpathia* sailed on towards New York. Word of the disaster was spreading not only in the city but also around the world. At first there were conflicting reports. Newspapers carried headlines claiming that the *Titanic* had sunk. Other headlines spoke of her striking an iceberg and calling for help. There were headlines too which claimed that all on board had been rescued and that the damaged ship was being towed into New York.

It was one of the first major disasters to capture worldwide attention. With radio and telephone communications, the news quickly spread to all corners of the globe. Most newspapers carried conflicting banner headlines about the disaster. A shocked public watched and waited.

On the *Carpathia*, Harold Bride had somewhat recovered from his ordeal and offered to help operate the radio. This he did while the liner continued her journey. Other survivors comforted their fellow passengers. Many, however, remained listless and depressed, haunted by what they had endured and what they had witnessed.

By Monday evening, official confirmation of what had actually happened was released to the public. A message to The White Star Line offices in New York, received earlier that day from the *Olympic*, conveyed the news that the *Titanic* had sunk with terrible loss of life.

There had been a delay in releasing this news. It was later claimed that this was done so that wealthy businessmen could protect their interests in the stocks of shipping and insurance companies. But like much else of the mystery surrounding the *Titanic*, this rumour was never proven.

On Thursday night, 18 April, *Carpathia* sailed into New York, past the Statue of Liberty, a potent symbol of the New World. Tens of thousands of people stood silently in the rain to watch.

By 9.30pm the survivors began to disembark. Many still remained silent. Others, however, were willing to speak to the many reporters gathered on the quay. It was in these reports that many of the legends and stories which still surround the great liner – her final hours and eventual sinking – were born.

The survivors told of both the bravery and cowardice shown by many of the crew and passengers. Some of these reports were true; others were pure fabrication. But perhaps after suffering such a trauma, the tellers of these tall tales could be forgiven their uncertainty about what they had witnessed.

There were claims that the iceberg had been sighted long before the collision; that officers had shot panicking passengers; that men had dressed up as women to escape the sinking ship; that a woman had refused to leave her beloved dog behind. Some undoubtedly were true. Others certainly were not. But why should truth stand in the way of a good story?

So the legend was born, guaranteeing that the public would continue to be fascinated by the *Titanic* long after she disappeared beneath the Atlantic. The reality of her conception, eventual demise and its significance for society were surely sufficient to guarantee the ship immortality anyway.

The sinking of the *Titanic* was to be a watershed. It created a dividing line between a time when everyone knew their place in society and the future seemed certain to a new era, where class structure was to be cast aside and man was to appear helpless in the face of nature.

The *Titanic*, with its three distinct classes, was a perfect example of society at the time. Each class knew its designated place and accepted this without question. So it was that a Third Class passenger on a sinking ship could be denied access to the boat decks because they would have to pass through a Second or First Class area. It was not simply that this was so but that everyone concerned accepted it. It was how people behaved towards each other.

Even as the boats were being loaded, class distinction was adhered to. No Third Class passenger would deem themselves worthy to share a boat with a passenger from First Class unless they were employed by the First Class person. And certainly no First Class passenger would accept that they should be asked to share a boat with a person of a lower class.

It is also obvious from the *Titanic* disaster that First and Second Class passengers were given priority in the lifeboats. On the other hand, those from Third Class were left to find their own way on deck. Although they were down in the lower decks and therefore needed most guidance, they were given little assistance. Some crew members did their best but on the whole the effort was too little and too late.

There is some evidence that many Third Class passengers, including women, were deliberately prevented from reaching the lifeboat decks. Just before the *Titanic* sank, Colonel Gracie claimed that he saw a large number of women emerge onto the boat deck at the stern.

He was shocked at this because he understood that all the women had got away in the lifeboats. But if, two hours after the ship struck the iceberg, a group of women from Third Class only then emerged onto the deck, it must have been because, in the previous two hours, they had been unable to do so. It would seem safe to assume that they had been prevented from coming on deck by locked gates or by crew members.

The evidence that is irrefutable is in the number of survivors. While there were 270 First Class passengers on board (this figure includes some personal servants like maids, valets, secretaries, etc.) 162 were rescued. The number of Third Class passengers on board was 710 but only 280 were rescued. These figures clearly show that priority was given to First Class passengers. One further stark statistic illustrates this. Despite Captain Smith's order that only women and children could take their place in the lifeboats, more First Class male passengers were rescued than children from Third Class.

At later inquiries into the disaster, these statistics were ignored, as was the reckless behaviour of Captain Smith. Despite the numerous warnings of icebergs, he did not slacken speed or set a new course to take the *Titanic* away from danger.

Captain Lord of the *Californian* was made a scapegoat for failing to come to rescue of the *Titanic*. Despite many appeals on his behalf, his name has never been cleared.

He was obviously negligent on the night of the disaster. But surely the blame for the large loss of life lies with Captain Smith, his officers and those who allowed a ship to sail without adequate lifeboat capacity.

This disaster would not occur again and new regulations were introduced. From then on ships were obliged to carry sufficient lifeboats to rescue all on board in the event of a disaster occurring. It also became compulsory for the radio to be manned on a round-the-clock basis. No longer would an operator sleep while a disaster was taking place just a few miles away.

While the sinking of the *Titanic* began a process of change in society, an event was about to take place that would hasten and complete that change. This was the First World War, which began two years after the sinking. By 1918, when it ended, millions of young men, mostly from the working classes, had died in Belgium and France, fighting in the trenches. These were, for the most part, the kind of men who would have travelled Third Class on the *Titanic*. Many people, horrified at the futile loss of life, began to clearly see the inequality in society and demanded change.

And change did come. While society was still divided into different classes by wealth, power and influence, the working classes were not willing to accept that they were of less value than those in the higher classes any more.

If the *Titanic* tragedy happened after the First World War, Third Class passengers would have regarded it as their right to enter the First Class sections in order to save their lives. And, more important still, First Class passengers would have accepted this.

The *Titanic* disaster, despite the great loss of life, did not bring an end to the era of luxury ocean travel across the Atlantic. But a new era and a new means of crossing the ocean were soon about to dawn. Man had now taken to the air and in the future this would become the most popular means of crossing the Atlantic.

In time air travel would replace the great, luxurious ocean-going liners. But it did not signal their death knell. Instead, they became floating luxury hotels for those who wished to savour the pleasure of sailing the oceans of the world, visiting far-flung and exotic places.

Many of these ships were bigger and even more luxurious than the *Titanic*. But none of them were to carry the same aura or fascination as the doomed ship. Nearly 100 years after she sank, she is still capable of capturing the imagination of young and old alike.

Like the *Santa Maria*, *The Golden Hind* and *The Victory*, her memory will live on in the minds of those who, thousands of years after man first dreamed of conquering the sea, still live in thrall to the tossing, restless oceans of the world.

THE WRECK IS FOUND

After the *Titanic* sank, many men dreamed of locating the wreck. Some were motivated by their fascination with the ship. Others, however, were motivated by greed.

After the sinking, rumours abounded that she had been carrying gold bullion. This was unlikely to be true but greed blinds men to reality. What was not in doubt was that there were many wealthy passengers on board, indeed some of the wealthiest people alive at that time.

Those like John Jacob Astor and his wife Madeleine, Isidor Straus and his wife Ida, and Benjamin

Guggenheim, were known for their fabulous wealth. A voyage on the *Titanic* was an opportunity to display this wealth in public, especially for the women on board.

They would have brought their valuable jewellery with them to wear at dinner and at gala concerts on the ship. When not being worn, such jewellery would have been kept in the ship's safe or in the safes in the First Class suites.

Now men dreamed of locating the wreck and salvaging the other valuable items kept in the safes. Over the years following the sinking, attempts were made to try and locate the wreck but without success. This was due to some confusion as to its exact location. But as well as that, the means of locating a wreck some 4,000 metres beneath the Atlantic Ocean were simply not available.

It was not until the 1980's that the sort of technology capable of locating such a wreck became available. This included highly sophisticated sonar and remote controlled underwater cameras.

An American, Dr Robert Ballard, and a Frenchman, Jean-Louis Michel, teamed up to try and locate the wreck. In August 1985, on board *Le Suroit,* they searched an area of around 150 square miles near the location calculated by Officer Boxhall on the fateful night.

Like some other previous attempts, bad weather hampered the search and no positive evidence of the site was found. The search was abandoned and only resumed at the end of that month.

This time, a US Navy research vessel, the *Knoor*, was involved. It carried two unmanned submersibles, the *Argo* and the *Angus*. These could operate at depths of over 6,000 metres and were ideal for the task.

Argo was equipped with sophisticated sonar and also with video cameras. It could be lowered into the water and towed by the *Knoor* while its sonar and cameras searched the seabed for any wreckage.

Again, they failed to find anything and despondency was beginning to set in. Ballard calculated that rather than locating the actual wreck, they had a better chance of locating the trail of debris the ship would have left in its wake as it sank. This, as it turned out, was the key to unlocking *Titanic*'s resting place.

Early on the morning of 1 September, objects began to appear on the video screens. Amidst whoops of success and relief, Ballard was summoned. He arrived in the control room just as the underwater camera sent up to the surface a picture of a ship's boiler.

They had found the wreck of the *Titanic*.

It was around 2am in the morning, very close to the actual time when the ship had sunk. It was a moment to reflect on what had occurred at this place on a cold April night just over 73 years before.

Aware of the significance of the find and also aware that below them lay the resting place of 1,503 men, women and children, the initial mood of celebration became tempered. Ballard and some of his crew went up on deck and stood quietly in the darkness, remembering those who had died.

But time was pressing and they only had a few days left. Also, the weather was deteriorating. As the cameras surveyed the wreck, one mystery about the sinking was resolved.

Eyewitness accounts had given two versions of the ship's final moments. Some claimed that she had gone under intact. Others claimed that she had split in two before she sank.

Now it became clear that the ship had split in two. What Ballard's team had found was the bow section, sitting upright on the seabed. As they searched the seabed itself, they located many objects from the ship, including crockery and bottles of wine.

Their time was up and they had to return to harbour. Large crowds and the world's media were waiting for them. A press conference was held and it was announced that the wreck had been located.

There was worldwide interest in the find and in the pictures of the wreck. Many now came forward with plans to raise the ship or salvage it. Others, like Ballard, wished that the wreck should never be disturbed.

He returned on a second expedition in 1986, taking a three-man submersible named *Alvin.* Now Ballard was able to dive on the actual wreck and see the bow section with the human eye. The bow was still intact but was being eaten away by rust.

On a subsequent dive, Ballard entered the ship through the giant hole left by the collapsing funnel. No human remains were discovered but some items of clothing were found.

A self-propelled video camera was now deployed and it was able to enter the ship. It even descended the grand staircase. A remote-controlled device fitted to the camera tried to open the door of the safe. But it remained firmly closed.

The camera also searched the seabed and located a trail of debris from the ship, including coal, which would have fuelled the furnaces.

The stern section was also located about 600 metres away. Here, the results of the implosions that had occurred as the stern sank were obvious to see. The decks and hull had been shattered and twisted by tremendously powerful forces.

Robert Ballard had found the wreck. His dream had now been achieved. He did not wish to disturb the scene or retrieve any of the objects, which littered the seabed or were still on board the ship. Neither did he wish for any section of the ship itself to be disturbed.

But others were less scrupulous. Now that the position of the wreck was known, many other salvage operations set about retrieving objects and parts of the ship. Around 2,000 objects were officially recovered.

Many were exhibited in museums around the world, including the world famous National Maritime Museum at Greenwich, England. Here, in the grounds, a memorial was dedicated to the memory of the *Titanic* and those who perished on that night of 15 April 1912.

The last words on the terrible disaster might be best left with Robert Ballard, the first man to see the great liner since her sinking. In describing her last resting place and the resting place of those 1,503 persons who died in the tragedy, he said: 'It is quiet and peaceful and a fitting place for the remains of this greatest of sea tragedies. May it forever remain that way and may God bless those found souls.'

THE END

Children of Stone

A long time ago, when the earth was made of stone, the people of Marn faced many dangers. Gaelen, the chief, decides to visit Sarnay where a more productive grain grows. He also seeks protection from invaders. But Marn is left open to other dangers. Gaelen's children Bolan, Alna and Vanu learn of this and flee across the country in search of their father. Will they be able to reach him in time?

ISBN: 978-1903464885 • Price €5.99 • PB • 2005

The Knock Airport Mystery

Pug Banzinni, the most feared criminal in America, is in prison in Dublin, about to be sent back to jail in his own country. When Kevin Dolan encounters Tiny and Slim, two henchmen of Pug's, little does he know his boring summer is going to become exciting very quickly. Kevin overhears them concocting a plan to rescue Pug. Will the children be able to outwit the crooks in time?

ISBN: 978-1903464878 • Price €5.99 • PB • 2005

The Boy Who Saved Christmas

Imagine Christmas ever needing to be saved? But when Santa Claus is kidnapped by arch-criminal Mister Carbuncle and his gang of crooks, it becomes necessary. Timmy Goodfellow, an orphan boy, learns of the plan. He sets out with his animal friends, including Beaky, Mousey, Mr Bull and Ratty, to find and rescue Santa. But time is running out. His courage is pushed to the limit. Will the most feared crook in the world destroy Christmas forever?

ISBN: 978-1903464182 • Price €5.99 • PB • 2004

Can Timmy Save Toyland?

When Santa learns Toyland is disappearing there is only one boy who can help; Timmy Goodfellow – *The Boy Who Saved Christmas*. Timmy appeals to grown-ups for help when he hears a hole in the ozone layer is causing the ice around Toyland to melt. But Timmy doesn't know Mister Carbuncle is up to his old tricks. To make matters worse, Katie, Timmy's little sister, is kidnapped and used as a hostage. Can Timmy save both Katie and Toyland?

ISBN: 978-1903464861 • Price €6.99 • PB • 2005

The Mulhern Twins
Mary Gallagher

Meet Dessie and Daisy, the Mulhern twins, two know-it-alls with a suspicious view of the adult world from the day they entered it. After their birth they discover life with slightly less-than-normal parents, Dottie and husband Bill, is going to be different.

ISBN: 978-1905172177 • Price € 5.99 • PB • 2006

The Snot Gang in 'Gotcha!'
Mary Gallagher

Holly is an ordinary kid trying to live her life in an ordinary way – by avoiding contact with adults as much as possible! When Holly has to do a school project about leprechauns she faces the improbable task of making people believe they exist, or else losing her street cred for good.

ISBN: 978-1903464717 • Price € 5.99 • PB • 2005

The Whiz Quiz Book
National Parents Council
REVISED EDITION

This quiz book was compiled by members of the National Parents Council (NPC) to meet demands from parents of primary schoolchildren. With 1,000 questions, this book offers endless scope and variety for parents, teachers and children to use free time gainfully and enjoyably.

ISBN: 978-1903464984 • Price € 5.99 • PB • 2005

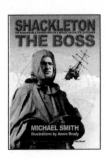

Shackleton: The Boss
The Remarkable Adventures of a Heroic Antarctic Explorer
Michael Smith

This inspiring story of Shackleton, whose men called him 'The Boss', involved four expeditions to Antarctica between 1901 and 1922. His incredible adventures included a breathtaking march to within a few miles of the South Pole and the amazing saga of hardship and survival on the famous *Endurance* expedition.

ISBN: 978-1905172276 • Price € 7.99 • PB • 2004

Tom Crean: Ice Man
The Adventures of an Irish Antarctic Hero
Michael Smith

Tom Crean was no ordinary man – he saved comrades from drowning in frozen waters, and rescued others from freezing snow, whilst following his leaders – Captain Scott and Ernest Shackleton, the famous Polar explorers.

ISBN: 978-1905172313 • Price € 7.99 • PB • 2003

Granuaile
Sea Queen of Ireland
Anne Chambers

Granuaile, a pirate queen and chieftain, ruled on land and sea in Connaught over 400 years ago. She loved the sea and became a better sailor than any of her father's crew. She had many adventures and escapades including a famous meeting with Queen Elizabeth I in London.

ISBN: 978-1905172108 • Price € 5.99 • PB • 2006